Slow Cooker
RECIPE COLLECTION

Publications International, Ltd.

Louis Weber, CEO
Publications International, Ltd.
8140 Lehigh Ave
Morton Grove, IL 60053

Pictured on the front cover *(clockwise from top left):* Twice "Baked" Potatoes *(page 168),* Mini Puttanesca Meatballs and Spaghetti *(page 134),* Salsa Verde Chicken Stew *(page 48),* Denver Egg Bowls *(page 10),* Orange and Pear Pork Roast *(page 94)* and Barbecued Beef Sandwiches *(page 190)*.

Pictured on the back cover *(clockwise from top left):* Maple, Bacon and Raspberry Pancake *(page 12)*, Black Bean, Zucchini and Corn Enchiladas *(page 161)*, Honey-Glazed Chicken Wings *(page 209),* Apricot and Brie Dip *(page 222),* Banana Pecan Bread Pudding *(page 233)* and Italian Meatball Hoagies *(page 187).*

ISBN: 979-8-89746-002-1

Manufactured in China.

8 7 6 5 4 3 2 1

Let's get social!
@Publications_International
@PublicationsInternational
www.pilbooks.com

Contents

Breakfast and Brunch

HAWAIIAN BREAD FRENCH TOAST

MAKES 8 TO 10 SERVINGS

- 6 eggs
- 1 cup milk
- 1 cup whipping cream
- 2 teaspoons coconut extract
- 2 teaspoons vanilla
- ¼ cup sugar
- 1 teaspoon ground cinnamon
- 1 pound sliced sweet Hawaiian bread or rolls
- 2 tablespoons butter, cut into ¼-inch pieces
- ½ cup large flaked or shredded coconut, toasted*

**To toast coconut, spread in single layer in small heavy skillet. Cook and stir over medium heat 3 to 4 minutes or until lightly browned and fragrant.*

1. Spray inside of slow cooker with nonstick cooking spray. Whisk eggs, milk, cream, coconut extract and vanilla in large bowl. Combine sugar and cinnamon in small bowl.

2. Layer bread slices in slow cooker, sprinkling each layer with cinnamon-sugar mixture. Pour egg mixture over top; press down bread to absorb egg mixture. Dot with butter. Cover and cook on HIGH 2 hours. Sprinkle with toasted coconut.

OVERNIGHT BACON, SOURDOUGH, EGG AND CHEESE CASSEROLE

MAKES 6 SERVINGS

- 1 loaf (about 12 ounces) sourdough bread, cut into ¾-inch cubes
- 8 slices bacon, chopped
- 1 large onion, chopped
- 1 red bell pepper, chopped
- 1 green bell pepper, chopped
- 2 teaspoons dried oregano
- ¼ cup sun-dried tomatoes packed in oil, drained and chopped
- 1½ cups (6 ounces) shredded sharp Cheddar cheese, divided
- 10 eggs
- 1 cup milk
- 1 teaspoon salt
- ¾ teaspoon black pepper

1. Spray inside of slow cooker with nonstick cooking spray. Place bread in slow cooker.

2. Cook bacon in large skillet over medium heat 5 minutes or until crisp, stirring occasionally. Transfer bacon to paper towel-lined plate using slotted spoon. Drain all but 1 tablespoon of drippings from skillet.

3. Heat same skillet over medium heat. Add onion, bell peppers and oregano; cook 5 to 7 minutes or until vegetables are softened, stirring occasionally. Stir in sun-dried tomatoes; cook 1 minute. Pour over bread in slow cooker. Stir in bacon and 1 cup cheese.

4. Whisk eggs, milk, salt and black pepper in large bowl; pour over bread mixture in slow cooker. Press down on bread to allow bread mixture to absorb egg mixture. Sprinkle remaining ½ cup cheese over top. Cover and cook on LOW 6 to 8 hours or on HIGH 3 to 4 hours. Cut into squares to serve.

CRANBERRY ORANGE SCONES

MAKES 6 SCONES

- ¼ cup (½ stick) cold butter
- 1 cup self-rising flour
- ¾ cup buttermilk
- 2 teaspoons granulated sugar
- 1½ teaspoons orange peel, divided
- ½ teaspoon ground cinnamon
- ¼ cup dried cranberries
- ¼ cup powdered sugar
- 1½ teaspoons orange juice
- ⅛ teaspoon salt

1. Cut one 16-inch piece of parchment paper; fold in half crosswise. Fit parchment paper into bottom and partly up sides of 1½-quart slow cooker. Spray parchment paper with nonstick cooking spray.

2. Grate cold butter into medium bowl on large holes of box grater. Add flour, buttermilk, granulated sugar, 1 teaspoon orange peel and cinnamon; stir until dry ingredients are just moistened. Fold in cranberries.

3. Turn out dough onto lightly floured surface. Knead four to six times or until dough forms a ball. Press into 6-inch disc; score into six wedges. Place dough into slow cooker on top of parchment paper.

4. Lay clean kitchen towel across top of slow cooker; cover with lid. Cover and cook on HIGH 1½ hours. Remove scones with parchment paper to wire rack.

5. Combine powdered sugar, orange juice, remaining ½ teaspoon orange peel and salt in small bowl; whisk until blended. Drizzle over scones; serve warm or at room temperature.

DENVER EGG BOWLS ▸

MAKES 4 SERVINGS

- 4 bell peppers, any color
- 10 eggs
- ¼ cup diced ham, plus additional for topping
- 3 green onions, chopped
- ½ teaspoon salt
- Black pepper
- 1 cup (4 ounces) shredded Cheddar cheese

1. Cut thin slice off top of each bell pepper; reserve tops. Carefully remove and discard seeds and membranes, leaving peppers whole. Dice bell pepper tops; measure ¼ cup. Trim bottoms of peppers so they stand up, if necessary.

2. Whisk eggs, ¼ cup diced bell peppers, ¼ cup ham, green onions, salt and black pepper in large liquid measuring cup until well blended. Pour egg mixture evenly into each bell pepper; place in slow cooker. Add water to slow cooker to come about three fourths of the way up peppers.

3. Cover and cook on HIGH 3½ hours. Sprinkle with cheese and additional ham, if desired.

BACON AND CHEESE BRUNCH POTATOES

MAKES 6 SERVINGS

- 4 slices bacon, chopped
- 3 russet potatoes (about 2 pounds), peeled and cut into 1-inch pieces
- 1 cup chopped onion
- ½ teaspoon seasoned salt
- 1 cup (4 ounces) shredded sharp Cheddar cheese
- 1 tablespoon water

1. Cook bacon in large skillet over medium heat 5 minutes or until crisp, stirring occasionally. Transfer bacon to paper towel-lined plate using slotted spoon.

2. Spray inside of slow cooker with nonstick cooking spray. Layer half of potatoes, onion, seasoned salt, bacon and cheese in slow cooker. Repeat layers. Sprinkle water over top.

3. Cover and cook on LOW 6 hours or on HIGH 3½ hours. Stir gently to mix and serve hot.

MAPLE, BACON AND RASPBERRY PANCAKE

MAKES 8 SERVINGS

- 5 slices bacon, chopped
- 2 cups pancake mix
- 1 cup water
- ½ cup maple syrup, plus additional for serving
- 1 cup fresh raspberries, plus additional for garnish
- 3 tablespoons chopped pecans, toasted*

**To toast pecans, spread in single layer in small heavy skillet. Cook and stir over medium heat 2 to 3 minutes or until lightly browned and fragrant.*

1. Cook bacon in large skillet over medium heat 5 minutes or until crisp, stirring occasionally. Transfer bacon to paper towel-lined plate using slotted spoon.

2. Brush inside of 5-quart slow cooker with 1 to 2 tablespoons drippings from skillet. Combine pancake mix, water and ½ cup maple syrup in large bowl; stir to blend. Pour half of batter into slow cooker; top with ½ cup raspberries, half of bacon and half of pecans. Pour remaining half of batter over top; sprinkle with remaining ½ cup raspberries, bacon and pecans.

3. Cover and cook on HIGH 1½ to 2 hours or until pancake is puffed and toothpick inserted into center comes out clean. Turn off heat. Remove cover; let stand 10 to 15 minutes. Remove pancake from slow cooker; cut into eight pieces. Serve with additional maple syrup and raspberries.

OVERNIGHT BREAKFAST PORRIDGE

MAKES 4 SERVINGS

- ¾ cup uncooked steel-cut oats
- ¼ cup uncooked quinoa, rinsed and drained
- ¼ cup dried cranberries, plus additional for serving
- ¼ cup raisins
- 3 tablespoons ground flax seeds
- 2 tablespoons chia seeds
- ¼ teaspoon salt
- ¼ teaspoon ground cinnamon
- 2½ cups almond milk, plus additional for serving
- Maple syrup (optional)
- ¼ cup sliced almonds, toasted*

**To toast almonds, spread in single layer in small heavy skillet. Cook and stir over medium heat 1 to 2 minutes or until nuts are lightly browned and fragrant.*

1. Combine oats, quinoa, ¼ cup cranberries, raisins, flax seeds, chia seeds, salt and cinnamon in heat-safe bowl that fits inside of 5- or 6-quart slow cooker.* Stir in 2½ cups almond milk.

2. Place bowl in slow cooker; pour enough water into slow cooker to come halfway up side of bowl.

3. Cover and cook on LOW 8 hours. Carefully remove bowl from slow cooker. Stir in additional almond milk, if desired. Top each serving with maple syrup, almonds and additional cranberries, if desired.

**A round soufflé dish or metal mixing bowl both work well.*

HASH BROWN AND SPINACH BREAKFAST CASSEROLE

MAKES 6 TO 8 SERVINGS

- 4 cups frozen Southern-style diced hash browns
- 3 tablespoons butter
- 1 large onion, chopped
- 1 package (8 ounces) sliced mushrooms
- 3 cloves garlic, minced
- 1 package (10 ounces) frozen chopped spinach, thawed and squeezed dry
- 8 eggs
- 1 cup milk
- 1 teaspoon salt
- ¼ teaspoon black pepper
- 1½ cups (6 ounces) shredded sharp Cheddar cheese, divided

1. Spray inside of slow cooker with nonstick cooking spray. Place hash browns in slow cooker.

2. Melt butter in large skillet over medium-high heat. Add onion, mushrooms and garlic; cook 5 to 7 minutes or until mushrooms have released their liquid and begin to brown. Add spinach; cook and stir 2 minutes or until mushrooms are tender. Stir into hash browns in slow cooker.

3. Whisk eggs, milk, salt and pepper in large bowl; until well blended. Pour over hash brown mixture in slow cooker. Sprinkle with 1 cup cheese.

4. Cover and cook on LOW 4 to 4½ hours or on HIGH 1½ to 2 hours or until eggs are set. Top with remaining ½ cup cheese; let stand until melted. Cut into wedges to serve.

ORANGE POPPY SEED CAKE

MAKES 8 SERVINGS

- 1½ cups biscuit baking mix
- ¾ cup granulated sugar
- 2 tablespoons poppy seeds
- ½ cup sour cream
- 1 egg
- 2 tablespoons milk
- 1 teaspoon vanilla
- 2 teaspoons orange peel
- ¼ cup orange juice
- 2 cups powdered sugar, sifted
- 2 teaspoons poppy seeds

1. Spray inside of 4-quart slow cooker with nonstick cooking spray. Cut waxed paper circle to fit bottom of slow cooker (trace insert bottom and cut slightly smaller to fit). Spray with cooking spray.

2. Whisk baking mix, granulated sugar and poppy seeds in large bowl. Whisk sour cream, egg, milk, vanilla and orange peel in medium bowl. Add to dry ingredients; stir just until blended.

3. Spoon batter into slow cooker; smooth top. Lay paper towels over top of slow cooker; cover with lid. Cook on HIGH 1 hour 30 minutes or until top is no longer shiny and a toothpick inserted in center comes out clean.

4. Invert cake onto plate. Peel off waxed paper and invert again onto wire rack. Cool at least 15 minutes.

5. For glaze, whisk orange juice into powdered sugar in medium bowl until smooth. Cut cake into eight wedges and place on serving plates. Drizzle glaze over tops; sprinkle with poppy seeds.

SAVORY SAUSAGE BREAD PUDDING

MAKES 4 TO 6 SERVINGS

- 4 eggs
- 2 cups milk
- ½ teaspoon salt
- ¼ teaspoon black pepper
- ¼ teaspoon dried thyme
- ⅛ teaspoon red pepper flakes
- 1 package (12 ounces) breakfast sausage links, cut into ½-inch pieces
- ¾ cup (3 ounces) shredded Cheddar cheese
- 2 cups day-old bread, cut into ½-inch cubes
- 1 tablespoon butter, softened

1. Whisk eggs in large bowl until blended. Stir in milk, salt, black pepper, thyme and red pepper flakes. Add sausage, cheese and bread; press bread into egg mixture. Let stand 10 minutes or until liquid is absorbed.

2. Butter 2-quart soufflé dish or baking dish that fits inside slow cooker. Pour sausage mixture into dish. Cover dish with greased foil.

3. Pour 1 inch hot water into slow cooker. Add baking dish. Cover and cook on LOW 4 to 5 hours or until toothpick inserted into center comes out clean. Remove dish from slow cooker and let stand 10 minutes before serving.

Soups and Stews

BUTTERNUT SQUASH, CHICKPEA AND LENTIL STEW

MAKES 6 SERVINGS

- 2 cups diced peeled butternut squash (½-inch pieces)
- 2 cups vegetable broth
- 1 can (about 15 ounces) chickpeas, rinsed and drained
- 1 can (about 14 ounces) fire-roasted diced tomatoes
- 1 cup chopped onion
- ¾ cup dried brown lentils, rinsed and sorted
- 1 teaspoon ground cumin
- 1 teaspoon ground coriander
- ¾ teaspoon salt
- Olive oil (optional)

1. Combine squash, broth, chickpeas, tomatoes, onion, lentils, cumin, coriander and salt in slow cooker.

2. Cover and cook on LOW 8 to 9 hours or on HIGH 4 to 4½ hours or until squash and lentils are tender. Drizzle with oil, if desired.

CHICKEN AND MUSHROOM STEW

MAKES 6 SERVINGS

- 1 ounce dried porcini mushrooms
- 1½ cups hot water
- 4 tablespoons vegetable oil, divided
- 2 medium leeks (white and light green parts only), halved lengthwise and thinly sliced crosswise
- 1 carrot, cut into 1-inch pieces
- 1 stalk celery, diced
- 6 boneless skinless chicken thighs (about 2 pounds)
- Salt and black pepper
- 12 ounces cremini mushrooms, quartered
- ¼ cup all-purpose flour
- 1 teaspoon minced garlic
- 1 fresh thyme sprig
- 1 bay leaf
- ½ cup dry white wine
- 1 cup chicken broth

1. Place dried mushrooms in small bowl; pour hot water over mushrooms. Let stand 15 minutes or until softened. Remove mushrooms from water; strain water through fine-mesh strainer and reserve. Chop mushrooms.

2. Heat 1 tablespoon oil in large skillet over medium heat. Add leeks; cook and stir 8 minutes or until softened. Transfer to slow cooker. Add carrot and celery.

3. Season chicken with salt and pepper. Heat 1 tablespoon oil in same skillet over medium-high heat. Working in batches, cook chicken 8 minutes or until browned on both sides. Transfer to slow cooker.

4. Heat remaining 2 tablespoons oil in same skillet. Add cremini mushrooms; cook 7 minutes or until mushrooms have released their liquid and begin to brown. Add porcini mushrooms, flour, garlic, thyme and bay leaf; cook and stir 1 minute. Add wine; cook until evaporated, stirring to scrape up browned bits. Add reserved soaking liquid and broth; bring to a simmer. Pour mixture into slow cooker.

5. Cover and cook on HIGH 2 to 3 hours. Remove and discard thyme sprig and bay leaf before serving.

NOTE

Serve a whole piece of chicken with each serving or remove chicken to bowl, shred with two forks and stir back into stew.

BROCCOLI CHEDDAR SOUP

MAKES 6 SERVINGS

- 1 large bunch broccoli
- 3 tablespoons butter
- 1 medium onion, chopped
- 3 tablespoons all-purpose flour
- ¼ teaspoon ground nutmeg
- ¼ teaspoon black pepper
- 4 cups vegetable broth
- 1 medium red potato, peeled and chopped
- 1 teaspoon salt
- 1 bay leaf
- 1½ cups (6 ounces) shredded Cheddar cheese, plus additional for garnish
- ½ cup whipping cream

1. Coarsely chop broccoli florets. Peel stem with vegetable peeler or paring knife and coarsely chop stem.

2. Melt butter in medium saucepan over medium heat. Add onion; cook and stir 6 minutes or until softened. Add flour, nutmeg and pepper; cook and stir 1 minute. Transfer mixture to slow cooker. Stir in broth, broccoli, potato, salt and bay leaf.

3. Cover and cook on HIGH 3 hours. Remove and discard bay leaf. Working in batches, place soup in food processor or blender; process until smooth (or use immersion blender). Pour soup back into slow cooker. Stir in 1½ cups cheese and cream until melted and smooth. Garnish with additional cheese.

CHICKEN RAMEN NOODLE BOWLS

MAKES 6 SERVINGS

- 1 tablespoon olive oil
- 1 pound boneless skinless chicken thighs
- 1 large yellow onion, peeled and halved
- 6 cups chicken broth
- 2 tablespoons soy sauce
- 4 green onions, divided
- 1 (1-inch) piece fresh ginger, sliced
- 1 clove garlic
- 6 ounces shiitake mushrooms, thinly sliced
- ⅓ cup hoisin sauce
- 8 ounces uncooked fresh ramen noodles*
- 3 hard-cooked eggs (recipe follows), cut in half lengthwise
- ½ red bell pepper, thinly sliced
- Chopped fresh cilantro

**Or cook 3 packages (3 ounces each) dried ramen noodles according to package directions, omitting seasoning packets.*

1. Heat oil in large skillet over medium-high heat. Add chicken; cook 8 to 10 minutes or until browned. Transfer chicken to slow cooker. Place onion halves in skillet cut side down; cook 4 to 5 minutes or until lightly charred. Place in slow cooker. Add broth, soy sauce, 2 green onions, ginger and garlic.

2. Cover and cook on LOW 6 to 7 hours or on HIGH 3 to 4 hours. Remove chicken to large cutting board; shred with two forks. Strain broth into large bowl. Discard solids; return broth to slow cooker. Stir in mushrooms and hoisin sauce. Cover and cook on HIGH 30 minutes.

3. Divide noodles and broth among six bowls. Top each serving with chicken, mushrooms, one egg half, bell pepper and cilantro. Chop remaining 2 green onions; sprinkle evenly over bowls.

HARD-COOKED EGGS

Fill medium saucepan with water; bring to a boil over high heat. Carefully lower eggs into water. Reduce heat to medium; boil gently 11 minutes (or 6 minutes for jammy yolks). Drain eggs; add cold water and ice cubes to saucepan to cool eggs. Peel eggs when cool enough to handle.

FRENCH ONION SOUP

MAKES 8 SERVINGS

- ¼ cup (½ stick) butter
- 3 pounds yellow onions, sliced
- 1 tablespoon sugar
- 2 to 3 tablespoons dry white wine or water (optional)
- 8 cups beef or vegetable broth
- 8 to 16 slices French bread
- 1 cup (4 ounces) shredded Gruyère or Swiss cheese

1. Melt butter in large skillet over medium-low heat. Add onions; cover and cook 10 minutes or until onions are tender and translucent.

2. Remove cover. Sprinkle sugar over onions; cook and stir 20 minutes or until onions are browned. Add onions and any browned bits to slow cooker. Pour wine into skillet, stirring to scrape up browned bits. Add to slow cooker. Stir in broth. Cover and cook on LOW 8 hours or on HIGH 6 hours.

3. To serve, preheat broiler. Ladle soup into individual ovenproof soup bowls on baking sheet. Top each with one or two bread slices and cheese. Broil until cheese is melted and bubbly.

VARIATION

Substitute 1 cup dry white wine for 1 cup of broth.

VEGETABLE SOUP WITH BEANS

MAKES 6 SERVINGS

- 4 cups vegetable broth
- 1 can (about 15 ounces) cannellini beans, rinsed and drained
- 1 can (about 14 ounces) diced tomatoes
- 16 baby carrots
- 1 medium onion, chopped
- 1 ounce dried oyster mushrooms, chopped
- 3 tablespoons tomato paste
- 2 teaspoons garlic powder
- 1 teaspoon salt
- 1 teaspoon dried basil
- 1 teaspoon dried oregano
- ½ teaspoon dried rosemary
- ½ teaspoon dried marjoram
- ½ teaspoon dried sage
- ½ teaspoon dried thyme
- ¼ teaspoon black pepper
- French bread slices, toasted (optional)

1. Combine broth, beans, tomatoes, carrots, onion, mushrooms, tomato paste, garlic powder, salt, basil, oregano, rosemary, marjoram, sage, thyme and pepper in slow cooker; stir to blend.

2. Cover and cook on LOW 8 hours or on HIGH 4 hours. Serve with bread, if desired.

MATZO BALL SOUP

MAKES 4 TO 6 SERVINGS

- 12 cups chicken broth
- 4 parsnips, sliced into ½-inch rounds
- 2 carrots, sliced into ½-inch rounds
- 3 leeks, sliced
- 1 onion, sliced
- 1 rotisserie chicken (optional)
- 1 tablespoon chopped fresh dill

MATZO BALLS

- 1¼ cups matzo meal
- 4 eggs
- ½ cup water
- 5 tablespoons butter, melted
- 1 small bunch fresh parsley, minced
- Salt and black pepper

1. For soup, combine broth, parsnips, carrots, leeks and onion in slow cooker. Cover and cook on LOW 8 to 10 hours or on HIGH 4 to 5 hours.

2. Meanwhile for matzo balls, combine matzo meal, eggs, water, butter and parsley in medium bowl until well blended. Season with salt and pepper. Roll 2-tablespoon portions into balls. Place on plate; cover and refrigerate 30 minutes to 1 hour.

3. Bring saucepan of salted water to a boil over medium-high heat. Add matzo balls; simmer 20 minutes. Transfer to plate with slotted spoon; refrigerate until needed.

4. Remove skin and bones from chicken, if using; cut chicken into bite-sized pieces. Add chicken, dill and matzo balls to soup. Cover and cook on HIGH 15 minutes or until heated through. Season with salt and pepper.

CELERY-LEEK BISQUE

MAKES 4 TO 6 SERVINGS

- 3 bunches leeks (3 pounds), trimmed and well rinsed*
- 2 cans (about 14 ounces each) vegetable broth
- 2 stalks celery, sliced
- 1 carrot, sliced
- 3 cloves garlic, minced
- 1 cup cream cheese with garlic and herbs
- 2 cups half-and-half, plus additional for garnish
- Salt and black pepper
- Fresh basil leaves (optional)

**Gritty sand can get between the layers of the leeks and can be difficult to see, so you may need to rinse them several times.*

1. Combine leeks, broth, celery, carrot and garlic in slow cooker. Cover and cook on LOW 8 hours or on HIGH 4 hours.

2. Working in batches, process soup in blender or food processor until smooth (or use immersion blender). Add cream cheese to last batch. Return to slow cooker. Stir in half-and-half. Season to taste with salt and pepper.

NOTE

For best flavor, cool to room temperature and refrigerate overnight. Reheat in large saucepan over medium heat before serving. Garnish with swirl of half-and-half and basil.

ROASTED TOMATO-BASIL SOUP

MAKES 6 SERVINGS

- 2 cans (28 ounces each) whole tomatoes, drained and juice reserved (about 3 cups juice)
- 2½ tablespoons packed dark brown sugar
- 1 onion, chopped
- 3 cups vegetable broth
- 3 tablespoons tomato paste
- ¼ teaspoon ground allspice
- 1 can (5 ounces) evaporated milk
- ¼ cup chopped fresh basil, plus additional for garnish
- Salt and black pepper

1. Preheat oven to 450°F. Line baking sheet with foil; spray with nonstick cooking spray. Arrange tomatoes on foil in single layer. Sprinkle with brown sugar; top with onion. Bake 25 to 30 minutes or until tomatoes look dry and are lightly browned. Let tomatoes cool slightly; finely chop.

2. Place tomato mixture, 3 cups reserved juice from tomatoes, broth, tomato paste and allspice in slow cooker; mix well. Cover and cook on LOW 8 hours or on HIGH 4 hours.

3. Add evaporated milk and ¼ cup basil; season with salt and pepper. Cover and cook on HIGH 30 minutes or until heated through. Garnish with additional basil.

CAULIFLOWER SOUP ▸

MAKES 8 SERVINGS

- 2 heads cauliflower, cut into small florets
- 8 cups vegetable broth
- 1 cup chopped celery
- 1 cup chopped onion
- 2 teaspoons salt
- 2 teaspoons black pepper
- 2 cups milk or whipping cream
- 1 teaspoon soy sauce

1. Combine cauliflower, broth, celery, onion, salt and pepper in slow cooker. Cover and cook on LOW 7 to 8 hours or on HIGH 3 to 4 hours.

2. Pour cauliflower mixture into food processor or blender; process until smooth (or use immersion blender). Add milk and soy sauce; process until blended. Pour soup back into slow cooker. Cover and cook on HIGH 15 to 20 minutes or until heated through.

LEEK AND POTATO SOUP

MAKES 4 TO 6 SERVINGS

- 6 slices bacon
- 5 cups shredded frozen hash brown potatoes
- 3 leeks,* cut into ¾-inch pieces
- 1 can (10½ ounces) cream of potato soup
- 1 can (about 14 ounces) chicken broth
- 2 stalks celery, sliced
- 1 can (5 ounces) evaporated milk
- ½ cup sour cream

**Gritty sand can get between the layers of the leeks and can be difficult to see, so you may need to rinse them several times.*

1. Cook bacon in large skillet over medium heat 5 minutes or until crisp. Transfer bacon to paper towel-lined plate using slotted spoon.

2. Combine potatoes, leeks, potato soup, broth, celery, evaporated milk and all but 2 tablespoons bacon in slow cooker. Cover and cook on LOW 6 to 7 hours.

3. Stir in sour cream. Sprinkle with reserved bacon.

Chilies

WHITE CHICKEN CHILI

MAKES 6 TO 8 SERVINGS

- 8 ounces dried navy beans, rinsed and sorted
- 1 tablespoon vegetable oil
- 2 pounds boneless skinless chicken breasts
- 2 onions, chopped
- 1 tablespoon minced garlic
- 2 teaspoons ground cumin
- 2 teaspoons salt
- 1 teaspoon dried oregano
- ¼ teaspoon black pepper
- ¼ teaspoon ground red pepper (optional)
- 4 cups chicken broth
- 1 can (4 ounces) fire-roasted diced mild green chiles, drained
- ¼ cup chopped fresh cilantro

1. Place beans in slow cooker. Heat oil in large skillet over medium-high heat. Add chicken; cook 8 minutes or until browned on all sides. Transfer to slow cooker.

2. Heat same skillet over medium heat. Add onions; cook and stir 6 minutes or until softened and lightly browned. Add garlic, cumin, salt, oregano, black pepper and ground red pepper, if desired; cook and stir 1 minute. Add broth and chiles; bring to a simmer, stirring to scrape up browned bits. Pour broth mixture into slow cooker.

3. Cover and cook on LOW 5 hours. Transfer chicken to large cutting board; shred with two forks. Return chicken to slow cooker. Serve with cilantro.

CORN CHIP CHILI

MAKES 6 SERVINGS

- 1 tablespoon olive oil
- 1 medium onion, chopped
- 1 red bell pepper, chopped
- 1 jalapeño pepper, seeded and finely chopped
- 4 cloves garlic, minced
- 2 pounds ground beef
- 1 can (4 ounces) diced green chiles, drained
- 2 cans (about 14 ounces each) fire-roasted diced tomatoes
- 2 tablespoons chili powder
- 1½ teaspoons ground cumin
- 1½ teaspoons dried oregano
- ¾ teaspoon salt
- 3 cups corn chips
- Shredded Cheddar cheese and chopped green onions

1. Heat oil in large skillet over medium-high heat. Add onion, bell pepper, jalapeño pepper and garlic; cook and stir 3 minutes or until softened. Add beef; cook and stir 10 to 12 minutes or until beef is no longer pink and liquid has evaporated. Stir in green chiles; cook 1 minute. Transfer beef mixture to slow cooker. Stir in tomatoes, chili powder, cumin, oregano and salt.

2. Cover and cook on LOW 6 to 7 hours or on HIGH 3 to 3½ hours. Place corn chips in serving bowls; top with chili. Sprinkle with cheese and green onions.

SWEET POTATO AND BLACK BEAN CHIPOTLE CHILI

MAKES 8 TO 10 SERVINGS

- 1 tablespoon vegetable oil
- 2 large onions, chopped
- 1 tablespoon minced garlic
- 2 tablespoons tomato paste
- 3 tablespoons chili powder
- 1 tablespoon chipotle chili powder
- 1 teaspoon ground cumin
- 2 teaspoons salt
- 1 cup water
- 1 large sweet potato, peeled and cut into ½-inch pieces (about 2 pounds)
- 2 cans (28 ounces each) black beans, rinsed and drained
- 2 cans (28 ounces each) crushed tomatoes
- Optional toppings: sour cream, sliced green onions, shredded cheddar cheese and/or tortilla chips

1. Heat oil in large skillet over medium-high heat. Add onions; cook 8 minutes or until lightly browned and softened. Add garlic, tomato paste, chili powder, chipotle chili powder, cumin and salt; cook and stir 1 minute. Add water, stirring to scrape up browned bits from bottom of skillet. Pour into slow cooker. Stir in sweet potato, beans and tomatoes.

2. Cover and cook on LOW 8 hours or on HIGH 4 hours. Serve with desired toppings.

SALSA VERDE CHICKEN STEW

MAKES 4 TO 6 SERVINGS

- 2 cans (about 15 ounces each) black beans, rinsed and drained
- 1½ cups thawed frozen corn
- 1 jar (24 ounces) salsa verde
- 1½ pounds boneless skinless chicken breasts
- ¾ cup chopped fresh cilantro
- Salt and black pepper
- Optional toppings: diced avocado, sour cream and/or tortilla chips

1. Combine beans, corn and ½ cup salsa in slow cooker. Arrange chicken over top; pour remaining salsa over chicken. Cover and cook on HIGH 2 to 3 hours or on LOW 4 to 6 hours.

2. Transfer chicken to cutting board; cut into bite-size pieces. Return chicken to slow cooker; stir in cilantro and season to taste with salt and black pepper. Serve with desired toppings.

TURKEY CHILI

MAKES 6 SERVINGS

- 2 tablespoons olive oil, divided
- 1½ pounds ground turkey
- 2 medium onions, chopped
- 1 red bell pepper, chopped
- 1 green bell pepper, chopped
- 5 cloves garlic, minced
- 1 jalapeño pepper, finely chopped
- 2 cans (about 14 ounces each) fire-roasted diced tomatoes
- 4 teaspoons chili powder
- 1 teaspoon ground cumin
- 1 teaspoon dried oregano
- 1 teaspoon salt

1. Heat 1 tablespoon oil in large skillet over medium-high heat. Add turkey; cook 7 to 8 minutes, stirring to break up meat. Transfer to slow cooker using slotted spoon.

2. Heat remaining 1 tablespoon oil in same skillet over medium-high heat. Add onions, bell peppers, garlic and jalapeño pepper; cook and stir 4 to 5 minutes or until softened. Transfer to slow cooker. Stir in tomatoes, chili powder, cumin, oregano and salt. Cover and cook on LOW 6 hours.

MOLE CHILI

MAKES 4 TO 6 SERVINGS

- 2 corn tortillas, each cut into 4 wedges
- 1½ pounds boneless beef chuck, cut into 1-inch pieces
- 1 teaspoon salt
- ½ teaspoon black pepper
- 3 tablespoons olive oil, divided
- 2 medium onions, chopped
- 5 cloves garlic, minced
- 1 cup beef broth
- 1 can (about 14 ounces) fire-roasted diced tomatoes
- 2 tablespoons chili powder
- 1 tablespoon ground ancho chile
- 1 teaspoon ground cumin
- 1 teaspoon dried oregano
- ¾ teaspoon ground cinnamon
- 1 can (about 15 ounces) red kidney beans, rinsed and drained
- 1½ ounces semisweet chocolate, chopped
- Queso fresco and chopped fresh cilantro (optional)

1. Place tortillas in food processor or blender; process to fine crumbs.

2. Season beef with salt and pepper. Heat 1 tablespoon oil in large skillet over medium-high heat. Add half of beef; cook 4 minutes or until browned. Place in slow cooker. Repeat with 1 tablespoon oil and remaining beef.

3. Heat remaining 1 tablespoon oil in skillet. Add onion and garlic; cook and stir 5 minutes or until softened. Pour broth into skillet, stirring to scrape up browned bits from bottom of skillet. Transfer to slow cooker. Stir in tortilla crumbs, tomatoes, chili powder, ancho chile, cumin, oregano and cinnamon.

4. Cover and cook on LOW 8 to 8½ hours. Stir in beans. Cover and cook on LOW 30 minutes. Turn off heat; stir in chocolate until melted. Top with queso fresco and cilantro, if desired.

HEARTY PORK AND BACON CHILI

MAKES 8 TO 10 SERVINGS

- 2½ pounds boneless pork shoulder, cut into 1-inch pieces
- 3½ teaspoons salt, divided
- 1¼ teaspoons black pepper, divided
- 1 tablespoon vegetable oil
- 4 slices thick-cut bacon, chopped
- 2 medium onions, chopped
- 1 red bell pepper, chopped
- ¼ cup chili powder
- 2 tablespoons tomato paste
- 1 tablespoon minced garlic
- 1 tablespoon ground cumin
- 1 tablespoon smoked paprika
- 1 bottle (12 ounces) pale ale
- 2 cans (about 14 ounces each) diced tomatoes
- 2 cups water
- ¾ cup dried kidney beans, rinsed and sorted
- ¾ cup dried black beans, rinsed and sorted
- 3 tablespoons cornmeal
- Feta cheese and chopped fresh cilantro (optional)

1. Season pork with 1 teaspoon salt and 1 teaspoon black pepper. Heat oil in large skillet over medium-high heat. Add pork in batches; cook 6 minutes or until browned on all sides, turning occasionally. Transfer to slow cooker using slotted spoon.

2. Heat same skillet over medium heat. Add bacon; cook and stir until crisp. Transfer to slow cooker using slotted spoon.

3. Pour off all but 2 tablespoons drippings from skillet. Heat skillet over medium heat. Add onions and bell pepper; cook and stir 6 minutes or just until softened. Stir in chili powder, tomato paste, garlic, cumin, paprika, remaining 2½ teaspoons salt and remaining ¼ teaspoon black pepper; cook and stir 1 minute. Stir in ale. Bring to a simmer, stirring to scrape up browned bits from bottom of skillet. Pour over pork in slow cooker. Stir in tomatoes, water, beans and cornmeal.

4. Cover and cook on LOW 10 hours. Turn off heat. Let stand 10 minutes. Skim fat from surface. Serve with cheese and cilantro.

THREE-BEAN CHILI WITH CHORIZO

MAKES 6 TO 8 SERVINGS

- 2 Mexican chorizo sausages (about 6 ounces each), casings removed
- 1 tablespoon vegetable oil
- 1 large onion, chopped
- 1 tablespoon salt
- 1 tablespoon tomato paste
- 1 tablespoon minced garlic
- 1 tablespoon chili powder
- 1 tablespoon ancho chili powder
- 2 to 3 teaspoons chipotle chili powder
- 2 teaspoons ground cumin
- 1 teaspoon ground coriander
- 3 cups water
- 2 cans (about 14 ounces each) crushed tomatoes
- ½ cup dried pinto beans, rinsed and sorted
- ½ cup dried kidney beans, rinsed and sorted
- ½ cup dried black beans, rinsed and sorted
- Chopped fresh cilantro (optional)

1. Heat large nonstick skillet over medium-high heat. Add sausage; cook 3 to 4 minutes, stirring to break up meat. Transfer to slow cooker using slotted spoon.

2. Heat oil in same skillet over medium heat. Add onion; cook and stir 6 minutes or until softened. Add salt, tomato paste, garlic, chili powders, cumin and coriander; cook and stir 1 minute. Transfer to slow cooker. Stir in water, tomatoes and beans.

3. Cover and cook on LOW 10 hours. Garnish each serving with cilantro.

TEXAS CHILI

MAKES 8 SERVINGS

- 3½ to 4 pounds cubed beef stew meat
- Salt and black pepper
- 4 tablespoons vegetable oil, divided
- 1 large onion, diced
- ¼ cup chili powder
- 1 tablespoon minced garlic
- 1 tablespoon tomato paste
- 1 tablespoon ground cumin
- 2 teaspoons ground coriander
- 1 teaspoon dried oregano
- 3 cans (about 14 ounces each) diced tomatoes
- 3 tablespoons cornmeal or masa harina
- 1 tablespoon packed brown sugar

1. Season beef with salt and pepper. Heat 3 tablespoons oil in large skillet over medium-high heat. Cook beef in batches 8 minutes or until browned on all sides. Transfer to slow cooker using slotted spoon.

2. Heat remaining 1 tablespoon oil in same skillet. Add onion; cook and stir 6 minutes or until softened. Stir in chili powder, garlic, tomato paste, cumin, coriander and oregano; cook and stir 1 minute. Stir in tomatoes, cornmeal and brown sugar; bring to a simmer. Transfer to slow cooker.

3. Cover and cook on LOW 7 to 8 hours. Season with additional salt to taste, if desired.

CLASSIC WEEKNIGHT CHILI

MAKES 6 SERVINGS

- 1½ pounds ground beef
- 1½ cups chopped onion
- 1 cup chopped green bell pepper
- 2 cloves garlic, minced
- 3 cans (about 15 ounces each) dark red kidney beans, rinsed and drained
- 2 cans (about 15 ounces each) tomato sauce
- 1 can (about 14 ounces) diced tomatoes
- 1 tablespoon chili powder
- 1 to 2 teaspoons hot dry mustard
- 1 teaspoon salt
- ¾ teaspoon dried basil
- ½ teaspoon black pepper
- 1 to 2 dried hot chile peppers (optional)
- Shredded Cheddar cheese and chopped fresh cilantro

1. Cook and stir beef, onion, bell pepper and garlic in large skillet over medium-high heat 6 to 8 minutes or until beef is no longer pink and onion is tender. Drain fat. Transfer to slow cooker.

2. Add beans, tomato sauce, diced tomatoes, chili powder, dry mustard, salt, basil, black pepper and chile peppers, if desired, to slow cooker; mix well.

3. Cover and cook on LOW 8 to 10 hours or on HIGH 4 to 5 hours. Remove and discard chile peppers before serving. Serve with cheese and cilantro.

HEARTY CHILI MAC

MAKES 4 SERVINGS

- 1 pound ground beef
- 1 can (about 14 ounces) diced tomatoes, drained
- 1 cup chopped onion
- 1 tablespoon chili powder
- 1 clove garlic, minced
- ½ teaspoon salt
- ½ teaspoon ground cumin
- ½ teaspoon dried oregano
- ¼ teaspoon red pepper flakes
- ¼ teaspoon black pepper
- 1 cup uncooked elbow macaroni

1. Brown beef in large skillet over medium-high heat, stirring to break up meat. Drain fat; place beef in slow cooker. Stir in tomatoes, onion, chili powder, garlic, salt, cumin, oregano, red pepper flakes and black pepper; mix well.

2. Cover and cook on LOW 4 hours.

3. Cook macaroni in medium saucepan of salted boiling water 2 minutes less than package directs for al dente. Drain and stir into slow cooker. Cover and cook on LOW 1 hour.

CHICKEN CHILI

MAKES 4 TO 6 SERVINGS

- 1 tablespoon vegetable oil
- 1½ pounds boneless skinless chicken thighs, cut into 1-inch pieces
- 1 large onion, chopped
- 1 red bell pepper, chopped
- 1 green bell pepper, chopped
- 4 cloves garlic, minced
- 2 cans (about 14 ounces each) diced tomatoes with mild green chiles
- 1 can (about 15 ounces) small white beans, rinsed and drained
- 1 can (8½ ounces) corn, drained
- 1 can (6 ounces) tomato paste
- 1½ tablespoons chili powder
- 1 teaspoon salt
- Optional toppings: shredded Cheddar cheese, minced chives and/or sour cream

1. Spray inside of slow cooker with nonstick cooking spray. Heat oil in large skillet over medium-high heat. Add chicken; cook and stir 5 to 6 minutes until lightly browned. Transfer chicken to slow cooker.

2. Add onion, bell peppers and garlic to same skillet; cook and stir 3 to 4 minutes or until softened. Transfer onion mixture to slow cooker. Stir in tomatoes, beans, corn, tomato paste, chili powder and salt.

3. Cover and cook on LOW 7 to 8 hours or on HIGH 3 to 4 hours. Serve with desired toppings.

Main Meats

PULLED PORK WITH HONEY-CHIPOTLE BARBECUE SAUCE

MAKES 8 SERVINGS

- 3 teaspoons chili powder, divided
- 1 teaspoon chipotle chili powder, divided
- 1 teaspoon ground cumin, divided
- 1 teaspoon garlic powder, divided
- 1 teaspoon salt
- 1 bone-in pork shoulder (3½ to 4 pounds), trimmed*
- 1 can (15 ounces) tomato sauce
- 5 tablespoons honey, divided

***If your slow cooker is smaller than 5 quarts, cut any roast larger than 2½ pounds in half so it cooks completely.*

1. Spray inside of slow cooker with nonstick cooking spray. Combine 1 teaspoon chili powder, ½ teaspoon chipotle chili powder, ½ teaspoon cumin, ½ teaspoon garlic powder and salt in small bowl. Rub spice mixture all over pork. Place pork in slow cooker.

2. Combine tomato sauce, 4 tablespoons honey, remaining 2 teaspoons chili powder, ½ teaspoon chipotle chili powder, ½ teaspoon cumin and ½ teaspoon garlic powder in large bowl. Pour tomato mixture over pork in slow cooker. Cover and cook on LOW 8 hours.

3. Transfer pork to large bowl; cover loosely with foil. Turn slow cooker to HIGH. Cover and cook on HIGH 30 minutes or until sauce is thickened. Stir in remaining 1 tablespoon honey. Turn off heat.

4. Remove bone from pork and discard. Shred pork using two forks. Stir shredded pork back into slow cooker to coat well with sauce.

POT ROAST WITH BACON AND MUSHROOMS

MAKES 6 SERVINGS

- 6 slices bacon, chopped
- 1 boneless beef chuck roast (2½ to 3 pounds), trimmed*
- ¾ teaspoon salt, divided
- ¼ teaspoon black pepper
- ¾ cup chopped shallots
- 8 ounces sliced white mushrooms
- ¼ ounce dried porcini mushrooms (optional)
- 4 cloves garlic, minced
- 1 teaspoon dried oregano
- 1 cup beef broth
- 2 tablespoons tomato paste
- Roasted Cauliflower (recipe follows, optional)

**If your slow cooker is smaller than 5 quarts, cut any roast larger than 2½ pounds in half so it cooks completely.*

1. Cook bacon in large skillet over medium heat 5 minutes or until crisp, stirring occasionally. Transfer bacon to paper towel-lined plate using slotted spoon.

2. Pour off all but 2 tablespoons drippings from skillet. Season roast with ½ teaspoon salt and pepper. Heat same skillet over medium-high heat. Add roast; cook 8 minutes or until well browned. Transfer to large plate. Add shallots, white mushrooms, porcini mushrooms, if desired, garlic, oregano and remaining ¼ teaspoon salt to same skillet; cook 3 to 4 minutes or until softened. Remove shallot mixture to slow cooker.

3. Stir bacon into slow cooker. Place roast on top of vegetables. Combine broth and tomato paste in small bowl; stir to blend. Pour broth mixture over roast. Cover and cook on LOW 8 hours.

4. Prepare Roasted Cauliflower, if desired. Transfer roast to large cutting board. Let stand 10 minutes before slicing. Top each serving with vegetables and cooking liquid. Serve with Roasted Cauliflower.

ROASTED CAULIFLOWER

Preheat oven to 375°F. Break 1 head of cauliflower into florets onto large baking sheet; coat with olive oil. Roast 20 minutes. Turn; roast 15 minutes.

CHEESEBURGER POTATO CASSEROLE

MAKES 6 SERVINGS

- 1 pound ground beef
- ½ cup chopped onion
- 1 can (about 10½ ounces) Cheddar cheese soup
- ¼ cup sweet pickle relish
- 2 tablespoons brown mustard
- 2 tablespoons ketchup, plus additional for topping
- 1 tablespoon Worcestershire sauce
- 1 package (30 ounces) shredded potatoes
- 1 teaspoon salt
- ½ teaspoon black pepper
- 2 cups (8 ounces) shredded Cheddar cheese
- Chopped green onions (optional)

1. Spray inside of slow cooker with nonstick cooking spray. Brown beef and onion in large skillet over medium-high heat 6 to 8 minutes, stirring to break up meat. Drain fat. Stir in Cheddar soup, relish, mustard, 2 tablespoons ketchup and Worcestershire sauce until well blended.

2. Arrange half of potatoes in bottom of slow cooker; sprinkle with ½ teaspoon salt and ¼ teaspoon pepper. Spoon half of meat mixture over potatoes and sprinkle with 1½ cups cheese. Top with remaining half of potatoes; sprinkle with ½ teaspoon salt and ¼ teaspoon pepper. Add remaining half of meat mixture; sprinkle with remaining ½ cup cheese.

3. Cover and cook on LOW 4 hours or on HIGH 2 hours. Top with additional ketchup and green onions, if desired.

SWEDISH MEATBALLS

MAKES 4 TO 6 SERVINGS

- 1½ pounds meatloaf mix*
- ¼ cup plain dry or panko bread crumbs
- 1 egg
- 1 teaspoon salt
- 1 teaspoon onion powder
- 1 teaspoon black pepper
- ¼ teaspoon ground allspice
- 1 cup beef broth
- 2 tablespoons Worcestershire sauce
- 2 tablespoons butter, melted
- 2 tablespoons all-purpose flour
- ¼ cup sour cream
- 1 tablespoon red currant jelly
- Hot cooked egg noodles
- Chopped fresh parsley (optional)

**Or substitute ¾ pound ground beef and ¾ pound ground pork.*

1. Combine meatloaf mix, bread crumbs, egg, salt, onion powder, pepper and allspice in large bowl; mix gently but thoroughly. Shape mixture into 24 (1-inch) balls. Refrigerate 1 hour.

2. Combine broth and Worcestershire sauce in slow cooker; add meatballs. Cover and cook on HIGH 5 hours.

3. Transfer meatballs to medium bowl using slotted spoon. Combine butter and flour in small bowl. Whisk half of butter mixture at a time into slow cooker until well blended. Combine sour cream and jelly in small bowl. Whisk half of jelly mixture at a time into slow cooker.

4. Cover and cook on HIGH 30 minutes or until sauce is thickened. Return meatballs to slow cooker; stir to coat. Serve over noodles. Garnish with parsley.

KALUA PIG ▸

MAKES 6 SERVINGS

- 3 slices bacon
- 1½ tablespoons coarse sea salt
- 1 boneless pork shoulder roast (5 to 6 pounds)
- 1 tablespoon liquid smoke
- Hot cooked rice
- Sliced green onions and chopped fresh cilantro

1. Line slow cooker with bacon. Rub salt generously over pork; place on top of bacon. Pour liquid smoke over pork.

2. Cover and cook on LOW 16 to 18 hours. Remove pork to large cutting board; shred with two forks. *Do not shred pork in cooking liquid.* Serve with rice, green onions and cilantro.

BACON AND ONION BRISKET

MAKES 6 SERVINGS

- 6 slices bacon, cut into ½-inch pieces
- 1 flat-cut boneless beef brisket (about 2½ pounds)
- Salt and black pepper
- 3 medium onions, sliced
- 2 cans (10½ ounces each) condensed beef consommé

1. Cook bacon in large skillet over medium heat 5 minutes or until crisp, stirring occasionally. Transfer bacon to slow cooker with slotted spoon.

2. Season brisket all over with salt and black pepper. Heat same skillet over medium-high heat. Add brisket; cook until browned on both sides. Transfer to slow cooker.

3. Heat same skillet over medium heat. Add onions; cook and stir 5 minutes or until softened. Add to slow cooker. Pour in condensed consommé. Cover and cook on HIGH 6 to 8 hours or until meat is tender.

4. Transfer brisket to cutting board and let rest 10 minutes. Slice brisket against the grain into thin slices. Season with salt and pepper, if desired. Spoon bacon, onions and cooking liquid over brisket to serve.

CLASSIC POT ROAST

MAKES 6 TO 8 SERVINGS

- 1 boneless beef chuck shoulder roast (3 to 4 pounds)*
- Salt and black pepper
- 1 tablespoon vegetable oil
- 6 medium red or yellow potatoes, cut into halves
- 6 carrots, cut into 2-inch pieces
- 2 medium onions, cut into quarters
- 2 stalks celery, sliced
- 1 can (about 14 ounces) diced tomatoes
- 1 teaspoon dried oregano
- 2 tablespoons water
- 1½ to 2 tablespoons all-purpose flour

**If your slow cooker is smaller than 5 quarts, cut any roast larger than 2½ pounds in half so it cooks completely.*

1. Season beef all over with salt and pepper. Heat oil in large skillet over medium-low heat. Add roast; cook until browned on all sides. Place in slow cooker.

2. Add potatoes, carrots, onions, celery, tomatoes, salt, pepper, oregano and enough water to cover bottom of slow cooker by about ½ inch. Cover and cook on LOW 8 to 10 hours.

3. Turn off heat. Remove roast and vegetables to large serving platter using slotted spoon. Let cooking liquid stand 5 minutes. Skim fat. Turn slow cooker to HIGH. Stir 2 tablespoons water into flour in small bowl until smooth; whisk into cooking liquid. Cover and cook on HIGH 10 to 15 minutes or until thickened. Season to taste with salt and pepper. Serve sauce over roast and vegetables.

SOUTH PACIFIC PORK RIBS

MAKES 4 TO 6 SERVINGS

- 3½ to 4 pounds pork loin riblets (about 20 riblets)
- Salt and black pepper
- 2 tablespoons vegetable oil, divided
- 1 onion, chopped
- 1 can (20 ounces) pineapple chunks packed in juice
- ¼ cup all-purpose flour
- ½ cup water
- ¼ cup rice vinegar
- ¼ cup packed brown sugar
- ¼ cup ketchup
- 1 tablespoon soy sauce

1. Season riblets with salt and pepper. Heat 1 tablespoon oil in large skillet over medium-high heat. Cook riblets in batches, turning to brown all sides and adding additional oil as needed. Transfer to slow cooker. Add onion to skillet; cook and stir 5 minutes or until softened.

2. Drain pineapple, reserving 1 cup juice. Whisk pineapple juice and flour in small bowl until well blended. Add water, vinegar, brown sugar, ketchup and soy sauce to skillet; cook and stir until smooth and well blended. Stir in juice mixture; cook over medium-low heat until thickened. Pour sauce over ribs in slow cooker; top with pineapple.

3. Cover and cook on LOW 8 to 10 hours or on HIGH 5 to 6 hours or until tender.

BEEF AND VEAL MEAT LOAF

MAKES 6 SERVINGS

- 1 tablespoon olive oil
- 1 small onion, chopped
- ½ red bell pepper, chopped
- 3 cloves garlic, minced
- 1 teaspoon dried oregano
- 1 pound ground beef
- 1 pound ground veal
- 1 egg
- 3 tablespoons tomato paste
- 1 teaspoon salt
- ½ teaspoon black pepper

1. Spray inside of slow cooker with nonstick cooking spray. Heat oil in large skillet over medium-high heat. Add onion, bell pepper, garlic and oregano; cook and stir 5 minutes or until vegetables are softened. Transfer mixture to large bowl; cool 5 minutes.

2. Add beef, veal, egg, tomato paste, salt and black pepper to onion mixture; mix gently but thoroughly. Shape into 9×5-inch loaf; place in slow cooker.

3. Cover and cook on LOW 5 to 6 hours. Remove meat loaf to cutting board; let stand 10 minutes before slicing.

PORK AND PINEAPPLE TERIYAKI ▸

MAKES 6 TO 8 SERVINGS

- 1 tablespoon vegetable oil
- 2 pork tenderloins (1¼ pounds each)
- 1 can (8 ounces) pineapple chunks packed in juice
- ½ cup teriyaki sauce
- 3 tablespoons honey
- 1 tablespoon minced fresh ginger
- Hot cooked rice

1. Heat oil in large skillet over medium-high heat. Add pork; cook 8 minutes or until browned on all sides. Place in slow cooker.

2. Combine pineapple with juice, teriyaki sauce, honey and ginger in large bowl. Pour over pork. Cover and cook on LOW 6 to 7 hours or on HIGH 3 to 4 hours. Transfer pork to cutting board; cover loosely with foil. Let stand 15 minutes before slicing.

3. Meanwhile, turn slow cooker to HIGH. Cook, uncovered, 10 to 15 minutes or until sauce is thickened. Serve pork with pineapple, rice and sauce.

CORNED BEEF AND CABBAGE

MAKES 6 SERVINGS

- 2 onions, thickly sliced
- 1 corned beef brisket with seasoning packet (about 3 pounds)
- 1 package (8 to 10 ounces) baby carrots
- 6 medium potatoes, cut into wedges
- 1 cup water
- 6 slices bacon, chopped
- 1 head green cabbage, cut into wedges

1. Place onions in slow cooker. Add corned beef with seasoning packet, carrots and potatoes. Pour 1 cup water over top. Cover and cook on LOW 10 hours.

2. With 30 minutes left in cooking time, cook bacon in large saucepan over medium heat 5 minutes or until crisp, stirring occasionally. Remove to paper towel-lined plate using slotted spoon. Reserve drippings in saucepan.

3. Place cabbage in saucepan with drippings; cover with water. Bring to a boil; cook 20 to 30 minutes or until cabbage is tender. Drain. Serve corned beef with vegetables; top with bacon.

SALISBURY STEAK

MAKES 4 SERVINGS

- 1 medium onion, sliced
- 1½ pounds ground beef
- 1 egg
- ½ cup seasoned dry bread crumbs
- 2 teaspoons Worcestershire sauce, divided
- 1 teaspoon ground mustard
- 1 can (10½ ounces) cream of mushroom soup
- ½ cup water
- 3 tablespoons ketchup
- ½ cup sliced mushrooms
- Chopped fresh parsley (optional)

1. Spray inside of slow cooker with nonstick cooking spray. Spread onion in slow cooker.

2. Combine beef, egg, bread crumbs, 1 teaspoon Worcestershire sauce and ground mustard in large bowl. Shape into four 1-inch-thick oval patties.

3. Heat large nonstick skillet over medium-high heat. Add patties; cook 2 minutes per side or until lightly browned. Transfer to slow cooker.

4. Stir soup, water, ketchup and remaining 1 teaspoon Worcestershire sauce in medium bowl. Pour mixture over patties; top with mushrooms.

5. Cover and cook on LOW 3 to 3½ hours. Garnish with parsley.

SERVING SUGGESTION

For a super easy meal, serve with prepared instant mashed potatoes and frozen peas.

BRAISED LAMB SHANKS

MAKES 4 SERVINGS

- 4 lamb shanks (12 to 14 ounces each)
- ¾ teaspoon salt, divided
- ¼ teaspoon black pepper
- 1 tablespoon olive oil
- 1 medium onion, chopped
- 2 stalks celery, chopped
- 2 carrots, chopped
- 6 cloves garlic, minced
- 1 teaspoon dried basil
- 1 can (about 14 ounces) diced tomatoes
- 2 tablespoons tomato paste
- Chopped fresh parsley (optional)

1. Spray inside of slow cooker with nonstick cooking spray. Season lamb with ½ teaspoon salt and pepper. Heat oil in large skillet over medium-high heat. Add lamb; cook 8 to 10 minutes or until browned on all sides. Place lamb in slow cooker.

2. Return skillet to medium-high heat. Add onion, celery, carrots, garlic and basil; cook and stir 3 to 4 minutes or until vegetables are softened. Add tomatoes, tomato paste and remaining ¼ teaspoon salt; cook and stir 2 to 3 minutes or until slightly thickened. Pour sauce over lamb in slow cooker.

3. Cover and cook on LOW 8 to 9 hours or until lamb is very tender. Remove lamb to large serving platter; tent with foil to keep warm. Turn slow cooker to HIGH. Cook, uncovered, on HIGH 10 to 15 minutes or until sauce is thickened. Serve lamb with sauce. Garnish with parsley.

PECAN AND APPLE-STUFFED PORK CHOPS

MAKES 4 SERVINGS

- 4 thick-cut bone-in pork loin chops (about 12 ounces each)
- 1 teaspoon salt, divided
- ½ teaspoon black pepper, divided
- 2 tablespoons vegetable oil
- ½ cup diced green apple
- ½ small onion, minced
- ¼ teaspoon dried thyme
- ½ cup apple brandy or brandy
- ⅔ cup cubed white bread
- 2 tablespoons chopped pecans
- 4 tablespoons frozen butter
- 1 cup unfiltered apple juice

1. Spray inside of slow cooker with nonstick cooking spray. Season pork chops with ½ teaspoon salt and ¼ teaspoon pepper. Heat oil in large skillet over medium-high heat. Add pork; cook 2 minutes per side or until browned. Place on cutting board.

2. Heat same skillet over medium heat. Add apple, onion, thyme, remaining ½ teaspoon salt and remaining ¼ teaspoon pepper; cook and stir 3 minutes or until onions are translucent. Add brandy; simmer until most of liquid is absorbed. Stir in bread and pecans; cook 1 minute.

3. Cut each pork chop horizontally to form pocket. Place 1 tablespoon butter into each pocket; divide stuffing among pork chops. Arrange pork chops in slow cooker, pocket side up.

4. Pour apple juice around pork chops. Cover and cook on HIGH 1½ to 1¾ hours or until pork is cooked though (145°F).

BACON, ONION AND STOUT BRAISED SHORT RIBS

MAKES 4 TO 6 SERVINGS

- 4 pounds bone-in beef short ribs, well trimmed
- Salt and black pepper
- 1 tablespoon vegetable oil
- 6 slices thick-cut bacon, chopped
- 1 large onion, halved and sliced
- 2 tablespoons all-purpose flour
- 2 tablespoons spicy brown mustard
- 1 tablespoon tomato paste
- 1 teaspoon salt
- ½ teaspoon black pepper
- 1 bottle (12 ounces) Irish stout
- 1 cup beef broth
- 1 bay leaf
- 2 tablespoons finely chopped fresh parsley
- Hot mashed potatoes or cooked egg noodles (optional)

1. Season ribs with salt and pepper. Heat oil in large skillet over medium-high heat until almost smoking. Cook ribs in batches, turning to brown all sides. Place in slow cooker. Wipe out skillet with paper towels.

2. Cook bacon in same skillet over medium heat about 5 minutes or until crisp, stirring occasionally. Transfer to paper towel-lined plate with slotted spoon. Drain all but 1 tablespoon drippings from skillet.

3. Heat same skillet over medium heat. Add onion; cook and stir 5 minutes or until softened. Add flour, mustard, tomato paste, 1 teaspoon salt and ½ teaspoon pepper; cook and stir 1 minute. Remove from heat; pour in stout, stirring to scrape up browned bits. Pour over ribs. Add bacon, broth and bay leaf to slow cooker.

4. Cover and cook on LOW 8 hours. Skim fat from cooking liquid. Remove and discard bay leaf. Stir in parsley. Serve with mashed potatoes.

HAM WITH SPICED COLA SAUCE

MAKES 10 TO 12 SERVINGS

- 1¼ cups packed dark brown sugar, divided
- ¾ cup cola, divided
- 3 tablespoons cider vinegar
- 1½ tablespoons grated orange peel
- 2 teaspoons ground cinnamon
- 1 teaspoon ground allspice
- 6 whole cloves
- ¼ teaspoon red pepper flakes
- 1 fully cooked bone-in ham (about 6 pounds)
- 2 tablespoons cornstarch

1. Combine 1 cup brown sugar, ½ cup cola, vinegar, orange peel, cinnamon, allspice, cloves and red pepper flakes in slow cooker; whisk until well blended. Place ham in slow cooker, cut side up. Cover and cook on LOW 5 hours or until ham is slightly separating from bone. Place ham on large cutting board. Cover and let stand 20 minutes.

2. Meanwhile, strain drippings into large measuring cup. Let stand 5 minutes; skim fat. Return drippings to slow cooker. Stir in remaining ¼ cup brown sugar.

3. Turn slow cooker to HIGH. Stir remaining ¼ cup cola into cornstarch in small bowl until smooth. Whisk into slow cooker. Cover and cook on HIGH 20 minutes or until thickened. Serve sauce with ham.

ORANGE AND PEAR PORK ROAST

MAKES 6 TO 8 SERVINGS

- ¼ cup pomegranate or cranberry juice
- ¼ cup sugar
- 1 tablespoon steak seasoning
- 2 teaspoons salt
- 2 teaspoons garlic salt
- 1 teaspoon black pepper
- 1 boneless pork roast (4 to 5 pounds)*
- 2 pears, cored and thickly sliced
- ½ unpeeled orange, thickly sliced

**If your slow cooker is smaller than 5 quarts, cut any roast larger than 2½ pounds in half so it cooks completely.*

1. Combine pomegranate juice and sugar in small saucepan; cook and stir over low heat 2 minutes or until sugar dissolves. Pour into slow cooker.

2. Combine steak seasoning, salt, garlic salt and pepper in small bowl. Rub mixture over roast. Place roast in slow cooker. Turn roast to cover with juice mixture; top with pear and orange slices.

3. Cover and cook on HIGH 6 to 8 hours. Transfer to cutting board; let stand 10 minutes. Slice and serve with sauce from slow cooker and fruit slices.

Poultry and Fish

RASPBERRY BBQ CHICKEN WINGS

MAKES 5 TO 6 SERVINGS

- 3 pounds chicken drummettes and wings, tips removed and split at joints
- Salt and black pepper
- ¾ cup seedless raspberry jam
- ½ cup sweet and tangy barbecue sauce
- 1 tablespoon raspberry red wine vinegar
- 1 teaspoon chili powder

1. Spray inside of slow cooker with nonstick cooking spray. Preheat broiler. Spray large baking sheet with cooking spray. Season chicken all over with salt and pepper. Arrange chicken on prepared baking sheet. Broil 6 to 8 minutes until browned, turning once. Place in slow cooker.

2. Combine jam, barbecue sauce, vinegar and chili powder in medium bowl; stir to blend. Pour sauce over chicken in slow cooker; turn to coat. Cover and cook on LOW 3½ to 4 hours. Place chicken on large serving platter; cover to keep warm.

3. Turn slow cooker to HIGH. Cook, uncovered, on HIGH 10 to 15 minutes or until sauce is thickened. Spoon sauce over chicken.

COCONUT-CURRY CHICKEN THIGHS

MAKES 4 SERVINGS

- 8 boneless skinless chicken thighs (about 2 to 2½ pounds)
- ½ teaspoon salt
- ¼ teaspoon black pepper
- 1 tablespoon olive oil
- 1 medium onion, chopped
- 1 red bell pepper, chopped
- 3 cloves garlic, minced
- 1 tablespoon grated fresh ginger
- 1 can (about 13 ounces) unsweetened coconut milk
- 3 tablespoons honey
- 1 tablespoon Thai red curry paste
- 2 teaspoons Thai roasted red chili paste
- ½ cup chopped cashew nuts (optional)
- 2 tablespoons chopped fresh cilantro (optional)

1. Spray inside of slow cooker with nonstick cooking spray. Season chicken with salt and black pepper. Heat oil in large skillet over medium-high heat. Add chicken; cook 6 to 8 minutes until browned on both sides, turning once. Remove to slow cooker.

2. Pour off all but 1 tablespoon drippings from skillet. Return skillet medium-high heat. Add onion, bell pepper, garlic and ginger; cook and stir 3 minutes or until vegetables begin to soften. Remove from heat. Stir in coconut milk, honey, curry paste and chili paste until smooth. Pour over chicken in slow cooker.

3. Cover and cook on LOW 4 hours. Serve chicken with sauce, cashews and cilantro, if desired.

SHRIMP JAMBALAYA

MAKES 8 SERVINGS

- 1 box (8 ounces) New Orleans style jambalaya mix
- 2½ cups chicken broth
- 1 can (about 14 ounces) diced tomatoes with green pepper, celery and onion
- 8 ounces andouille sausage, cut into ¼-inch-thick slices
- 1 teaspoon hot pepper sauce
- 1½ pounds large raw shrimp, peeled and deveined (with tails on)

1. Spray inside of slow cooker with nonstick cooking spray. Add jambalaya mix, broth, tomatoes, sausage and hot pepper sauce; stir to blend. Cover and cook on LOW 2½ to 3 hours or until rice is cooked through.

2. Stir in shrimp. Cover and cook on LOW 30 minutes or until shrimp are pink and opaque.

CHILI TURKEY LOAF

MAKES 8 SERVINGS

- 2 pounds ground turkey
- 1 cup chopped onion
- ⅔ cup Italian-style seasoned dry bread crumbs
- ½ cup chopped green bell pepper
- ½ cup chili sauce
- 2 eggs, lightly beaten
- 2 tablespoons horseradish mustard
- 4 cloves garlic, minced
- 1 teaspoon salt
- ½ teaspoon Italian seasoning
- ¼ teaspoon black pepper
- Salsa (optional)

1. Make foil handles (see below). Combine turkey, onion, bread crumbs, bell pepper, chili sauce, eggs, mustard, garlic, salt, Italian seasoning and pepper in large bowl; mix well. Shape into round loaf; place on foil strips in slow cooker.

2. Cover and cook on LOW 5 to 6 hours. Remove loaf from slow cooker using foil handles. Let stand 5 minutes. Cut into wedges; top with salsa, if desired.

FOIL HANDLES

Tear off three 18×2-inch strips of heavy foil or use regular foil folded to double thickness. Crisscross foil strips in spoke design and place in slow cooker to allow for easy removal of turkey loaf.

MISO-POACHED SALMON

MAKES 6 SERVINGS

- 1½ cups water
- 2 green onions, cut into 2-inch pieces
- ¼ cup yellow miso paste
- ¼ cup soy sauce
- 2 tablespoons sake
- 2 tablespoons mirin
- 1½ teaspoons grated fresh ginger
- 1 teaspoon minced garlic
- 6 salmon fillets (4 ounces each)
- Hot cooked rice
- Thinly sliced green onions

1. Combine water, 2 green onions, miso paste, soy sauce, sake, mirin, ginger and garlic in slow cooker; stir to blend. Cover and cook on HIGH 30 minutes.

2. Turn slow cooker to LOW. Add salmon, skin side down. Cover and cook on LOW 30 to 60 minutes or until salmon turns opaque and flakes easily with fork. Serve with rice and cooking liquid. Garnish with sliced green onions.

PINEAPPLE SALSA CHICKEN

MAKES 4 SERVINGS

- 1 medium onion, sliced
- 4 boneless skinless chicken breasts (6 to 8 ounces each)
- 1½ teaspoons salt
- ½ teaspoon onion powder
- ½ teaspoon garlic powder
- 1 teaspoon black pepper
- 1 jar (16 ounces) salsa
- 1 green bell pepper, sliced
- 1 can (20 ounces) pineapple chunks packed in juice
- 1 tablespoon cornstarch
- Hot cooked rice
- Lime wedges and chopped fresh cilantro (optional)

1. Place onion and chicken in slow cooker; season with salt, onion powder, garlic powder and black pepper. Top with salsa and bell pepper. Cover and cook on HIGH 4 hours.

2. Place chicken on large cutting board; shred with two forks. Skim fat from cooking liquid. Add pineapple with juice to slow cooker.

3. Stir ¼ cup cooking liquid into cornstarch in small bowl until smooth. Stir cornstarch mixture into slow cooker. Cover and cook on HIGH 15 minutes or until sauce is thickened and pineapple is heated through.

4. Stir shredded chicken back into slow cooker. Serve over rice with lime wedges and cilantro.

CARIBBEAN JERK CHICKEN

MAKES 6 SERVINGS

- 6 boneless skinless chicken thighs
- 1 small yellow onion, coarsely chopped
- ¼ cup chicken broth
- ¼ cup soy sauce
- 1 large jalapeño pepper, seeded
- 2 teaspoons minced garlic
- 1 teaspoon ground ginger
- 1 teaspoon dried thyme
- ½ teaspoon salt
- ¼ teaspoon ground cloves
- ⅛ teaspoon ground allspice
- ⅛ teaspoon ground cinnamon
- Hot cooked rice
- Thinly sliced jalapeño peppers (optional)

1. Spray inside of slow cooker with nonstick cooking spray; add chicken.

2. Combine onion, broth, soy sauce, whole jalapeño, garlic, ginger, thyme, salt, cloves, allspice and cinnamon in food processor or blender; process until well blended. Pour over chicken in slow cooker.

3. Cover and cook on HIGH 3 hours. Serve with rice and sliced jalapeños, if desired.

CHICKEN VESUVIO

MAKES 4 TO 6 SERVINGS

- 3 tablespoons all-purpose flour
- 1½ teaspoons dried oregano
- 1 teaspoon salt
- ½ teaspoon black pepper
- 1 whole chicken (about 4 pounds), cut up
- 2 tablespoons olive oil
- 4 baking potatoes, cut into wedges
- 2 onions, cut into thin wedges
- 4 cloves garlic, minced
- ¼ cup chicken broth
- ¼ cup dry white wine
- ¼ cup chopped fresh parsley

1. Combine flour, oregano, salt and pepper in large resealable food storage bag. Add several pieces of chicken to bag; shake to coat. Repeat with remaining chicken.

2. Heat oil in large skillet over medium heat. Add chicken; cook 10 to 12 minutes or until browned on all sides, turning occasionally.

3. Place potatoes, onions and garlic in slow cooker. Add broth and wine. Top with chicken pieces; pour pan juices from skillet over chicken. Cover and cook on LOW 6 to 7 hours or on HIGH 3 to 3½ hours or until chicken is cooked through and potatoes are tender.

4. Serve chicken and vegetables with juices from slow cooker; sprinkle with parsley.

SALMON COOKED IN BEER

MAKES 4 SERVINGS

- 4 salmon fillets (6 ounces each)
- Salt and black pepper
- 1 cup Italian salad dressing
- 3 tablespoons olive oil
- 1 yellow bell pepper, sliced
- 1 red bell pepper, sliced
- 1 orange bell pepper, sliced
- 1 large onion, sliced
- ½ teaspoon dried basil
- 2 cloves garlic, minced
- 1 teaspoon lemon peel
- 2 cups stemmed spinach
- ¾ cup amber ale
- ½ lemon, cut into quarters

1. Season both sides of salmon with salt and black pepper. Place in baking dish and pour Italian dressing over salmon. Cover and refrigerate 30 minutes or up to 2 hours. Discard marinade.

2. Pour oil into slow cooker. Arrange salmon in slow cooker, overlapping as necessary. Top with peppers, onion, basil, garlic and lemon peel. Cover with spinach. Pour beer over top. Cover and cook on HIGH 1½ hours.

3. Place salmon on plates; top with vegetables. Squeeze lemon over salmon and season with additional salt and pepper, if desired.

PINEAPPLE AND BUTTERNUT SQUASH BRAISED CHICKEN

MAKES 4 SERVINGS

- 1 medium butternut squash, cut into 1-inch pieces (about 3 cups)
- 1 can (20 ounces) pineapple chunks packed in juice
- ½ cup ketchup
- 2 tablespoons packed brown sugar
- 8 boneless skinless chicken thighs (about 2 pounds)
- ½ teaspoon salt
- ¼ teaspoon black pepper

1. Spray inside of slow cooker with nonstick cooking spray. Combine squash, pineapple with juice, ketchup and brown sugar in slow cooker; stir to blend. Season chicken with salt and pepper. Place chicken on top of squash mixture.

2. Cover and cook on LOW 5 to 6 hours. Place chicken on cutting board; cover loosely with foil. Turn slow cooker to HIGH. Cook, uncovered, 10 to 15 minutes or until sauce is thickened. Serve squash, pineapple and sauce over chicken.

EASY CHEESY BBQ CHICKEN ▸

MAKES 6 SERVINGS

- 6 boneless skinless chicken breasts (6 to 8 ounces each)
- 1 bottle (26 ounces) barbecue sauce
- 6 slices bacon, cut in half
- 6 slices (1 ounce each) Swiss cheese

1. Place chicken in slow cooker. Cover with barbecue sauce. Cover and cook on LOW 8 to 9 hours.

2. Cook bacon in large skillet over medium heat 5 minutes or until crisp, turning occasionally. Transfer bacon to paper towel-lined plate using slotted spoon.

3. Place two slices of cooked bacon over each piece of chicken in slow cooker. Top with cheese slices. Turn slow cooker to HIGH. Cover and cook on HIGH until cheese melts.

PROVENÇAL LEMON AND OLIVE CHICKEN

MAKES 8 SERVINGS

- 2 cups chopped onions
- 8 boneless skinless chicken thighs (about 2½ pounds)
- 1 lemon, thinly sliced and seeded
- 1 cup pitted green olives
- 1 tablespoon olive brine or white vinegar
- 2 teaspoons herbes de Provence
- 1 bay leaf
- ½ teaspoon salt
- ⅛ teaspoon black pepper
- 1 cup chicken broth
- ½ cup minced fresh parsley

1. Place onions in slow cooker; top with chicken and lemon slices. Add olives, brine, herbes de Provence, bay leaf, salt and pepper. Pour in broth.

2. Cover and cook on LOW 5 to 6 hours or on HIGH 3 to 3½ hours. Remove and discard bay leaf. Stir in parsley before serving.

TUNA CASSEROLE

MAKES 4 SERVINGS

- 2 cans (12 ounces each) solid albacore tuna, drained and flaked
- 3 cups diced celery
- 3 cups crushed potato chips, divided
- 6 hard-cooked eggs (page 28), chopped
- 1 can (10½ ounces) cream of mushroom soup
- 1 can (10½ ounces) cream of celery soup
- 1 cup mayonnaise
- 1 teaspoon dried tarragon
- 1 teaspoon black pepper

1. Spray inside of slow cooker with nonstick cooking spray. Combine tuna, celery, 2½ cups potato chips, eggs, soups, mayonnaise, tarragon and pepper in slow cooker; stir well.

2. Cover and cook on LOW 5 to 8 hours. Sprinkle with remaining ½ cup potato chips.

HERBED CHICKEN IN CREAM SAUCE

MAKES 4 SERVINGS

- 4 bone-in skinless chicken breasts (about 3 pounds total)
- ½ cup dry white wine, divided
- 1 tablespoon Italian salad dressing and seasoning mix
- ½ teaspoon dried oregano
- 1 can (10½ ounces) cream of chicken soup
- 3 ounces cream cheese, softened and cut into cubes
- ¼ teaspoon salt
- ⅛ teaspoon black pepper
- 2 tablespoons chopped fresh parsley

1. Spray inside of slow cooker with nonstick cooking spray. Arrange chicken in single layer in slow cooker, overlapping slightly. Pour ¼ cup wine over chicken. Sprinkle evenly with salad dressing mix and oregano. Cover and cook on LOW 5 to 6 hours or on HIGH 3 hours.

2. Place chicken on plate. Whisk soup, cream cheese, salt and pepper into cooking liquid. (Mixture will be a bit lumpy.) Arrange chicken on top. Cover and cook on HIGH 15 to 20 minutes or until heated through.

3. Place chicken on serving plates. Add remaining ¼ cup wine to sauce; whisk until smooth. Spoon sauce around chicken. Garnish with parsley.

HAM AND SAGE STUFFED CORNISH HENS

MAKES 4 SERVINGS

1¼ cups sliced celery, divided

1 cup sliced leeks

2 tablespoons butter, divided

¼ cup finely diced onion

¼ cup diced smoked ham or prosciutto

1 cup herb-seasoned stuffing mix

1 cup chicken broth

1 tablespoon finely chopped fresh sage *or* 1 teaspoon ground sage

4 Cornish hens (about 1½ pounds each)

Salt and black pepper

1. Spray inside of slow cooker with nonstick cooking spray. Add 1 cup celery and leeks.

2. Melt 1 tablespoon butter in large nonstick skillet over medium heat. Add remaining ¼ cup celery, onion and ham; cook and stir 5 minutes or until onion is translucent. Stir in stuffing mix, broth and sage. Transfer mixture to medium bowl.

3. Rinse hens and pat dry; sprinkle with salt and pepper. Spoon stuffing into cavities; tie drumsticks together with kitchen twine.

4. Melt remaining 1 tablespoon butter in same skillet over medium-high heat. Add two hens; cook until browned on all sides, turning occasionally. Transfer to slow cooker. Repeat with remaining hens.

5. Cover and cook on LOW 5 to 6 hours or on HIGH 3 to 4 hours. Remove and discard twine. Place hens on serving platter with vegetables; spoon broth over hens.

CARIBBEAN SHRIMP WITH RICE ▸

MAKES 4 SERVINGS

- 1 package (12 ounces) frozen large raw shrimp, thawed (with tails on)
- ½ cup chicken broth
- 1 clove garlic, minced
- 1 teaspoon chili powder
- ½ teaspoon salt
- ½ teaspoon dried oregano
- 1 cup frozen peas, thawed
- ½ cup diced tomatoes
- 2 cups cooked rice

1. Combine shrimp, broth, garlic, chili powder, salt and oregano in slow cooker. Cover and cook on LOW 2 hours.

2. Stir in peas and tomatoes. Cover and cook on LOW 5 minutes. Stir in rice; cover and cook on LOW 5 minutes or until heated through.

ASIAN BARBECUE SKEWERS

MAKES 4 TO 6 SERVINGS

- 2 pounds boneless skinless chicken thighs
- ½ cup soy sauce
- ⅓ cup packed brown sugar
- 2 tablespoons toasted sesame oil
- 3 cloves garlic, minced
- ½ cup thinly sliced green onions
- 1 tablespoon toasted sesame seeds

1. Cut each thigh into four pieces about 1½ inches wide. Thread chicken onto 7-inch wooden skewers, folding thinner pieces, if necessary. Place skewers in slow cooker, layering as flat as possible.

2. Whisk soy sauce, brown sugar, oil and garlic in small bowl. Reserve ⅓ cup sauce in small bowl; pour remaining sauce over skewers. Cover and cook on LOW 2 hours. Turn skewers; cover and cook on LOW 1 hour.

3. Place skewers on serving platter; pour reserved sauce over skewers. Sprinkle with green onions and sesame seeds.

BASQUE CHICKEN WITH PEPPERS

MAKES 4 TO 6 SERVINGS

- 1 whole chicken (about 4 pounds), cut into 8 pieces
- Salt and black pepper
- 1½ tablespoons olive oil
- 1 onion, chopped
- 2 cloves garlic, minced
- 3 bell peppers (red, yellow and green), cut into strips
- 1 package (8 ounces) cremini mushrooms, halved
- 1 can (about 14 ounces) stewed tomatoes
- ½ cup chicken broth
- ½ cup red wine
- 3 tablespoons tomato paste
- 1 fresh marjoram sprig (optional)
- 1 teaspoon salt
- 1 teaspoon smoked paprika
- ½ teaspoon black pepper
- 4 ounces diced prosciutto
- Hot cooked rice pilaf mix

1. Season chicken all over with salt and black pepper. Heat oil in large skillet over medium-high heat. Working in batches, brown chicken on all sides. Transfer to slow cooker.

2. Heat same skillet over medium-low heat. Add onions and garlic; cook and stir 3 minutes or until softened. Add peppers and mushrooms; cook and stir 3 minutes. Add tomatoes, broth, wine, tomato paste, marjoram, if desired, salt, paprika and black pepper; simmer 3 to 4 minutes. Pour over chicken in slow cooker. Cover and cook on LOW 5 to 6 hours or on HIGH 4 hours or until chicken is cooked through.

3. Transfer chicken to serving platter. Ladle vegetables and sauce over chicken. Sprinkle with prosciutto and serve with rice.

EASY HERBED TURKEY BREAST ▸

MAKES 4 TO 6 SERVINGS

- 1 boneless turkey breast (about 3 pounds)
- Salt and black pepper
- Garlic powder
- Paprika
- Dried parsley flakes

1. Place turkey in slow cooker. Season with salt, pepper, garlic powder, paprika and parsley flakes. Cover and cook on LOW 6 to 8 hours or until internal temperature reaches 170°F.

2. Place turkey on cutting board; cover with foil and let stand 10 to 15 minutes before carving. (Internal temperature will rise 5° to 10°F during stand time.)

CHICKEN AND STUFFING DINNER

MAKES 4 SERVINGS

- 1 can (10½ ounces) cream of chicken soup
- ⅓ cup milk
- 4 boneless skinless chicken breasts (6 to 8 ounces each)
- 1 package (6 ounces) stuffing mix
- 1⅔ cups water

1. Combine soup and milk in slow cooker; stir to blend. Add chicken.

2. Combine stuffing mix and water in large bowl; stir to blend. Spoon stuffing over chicken. Cover and cook on LOW 6 to 8 hours.

Pasta and Grains

HOMESTYLE MAC AND CHEESE

MAKES 6 TO 8 SERVINGS

12 ounces uncooked elbow macaroni (about 3 cups)

2 cans (12 ounces each) evaporated milk

1 cup milk

⅓ cup all-purpose flour

¼ cup (½ stick) butter, melted

2 eggs

1 teaspoon ground mustard

½ teaspoon salt

¼ teaspoon black pepper

4 cups (16 ounces) shredded sharp Cheddar cheese

Toasted plain dry bread crumbs (optional)

1. Cook pasta in large saucepan of salted boiling water 2 minutes less than package directs for al dente. Drain and place in slow cooker.

2. Whisk evaporated milk, milk, flour, butter, eggs, ground mustard, salt and pepper in large bowl until well blended. Pour into slow cooker. Stir in cheese.

3. Cover and cook on LOW 3½ to 4 hours or until cheese is melted and macaroni is heated through. Stir well. Top each serving with bread crumbs, if desired.

QUINOA PILAF WITH SHALLOT VINAIGRETTE

MAKES 6 SERVINGS

- 2 cups vegetable broth
- 1 cup uncooked quinoa, rinsed under cold water in fine-mesh strainer
- 2 stalks celery, finely chopped
- 1 carrot, finely chopped
- ½ red onion, finely chopped
- ¼ teaspoon dried thyme
- 1 shallot, chopped
- 1 tablespoon white wine vinegar
- 2 teaspoons honey
- 1 teaspoon Dijon mustard
- ½ teaspoon salt
- ⅛ teaspoon black pepper
- ¼ cup olive oil
- Chopped fresh parsley (optional)

1. Combine broth, quinoa, celery, carrot, onion and thyme in slow cooker. Cover and cook on HIGH 2 to 3 hours or until liquid is absorbed.

2. Meanwhile, combine shallot, vinegar, honey, mustard, salt and pepper in small bowl; whisk in oil. Fluff quinoa with fork; stir in shallot mixture. Garnish with parsley.

MINI PUTTANESCA MEATBALLS AND SPAGHETTI

MAKES 4 SERVINGS

- 1 pound ground turkey or ground beef
- ¼ cup seasoned dry bread crumbs
- 1 egg
- 1 jar (24 to 26 ounces) marinara sauce
- ½ cup coarsely chopped pitted kalamata olives
- 2 tablespoons drained capers
- ½ to ¾ teaspoon red pepper flakes
- 8 ounces uncooked spaghetti
- Slivered fresh basil or chopped fresh parsley (optional)

1. Preheat oven to 425°F. Combine turkey, bread crumbs and egg in large bowl; mix well. Shape into 24 (1-inch) meatballs; place on foil-lined baking sheet. Bake 15 to 18 minutes or until browned and no longer pink in center.

2. Combine marinara sauce, olives, capers and red pepper flakes in slow cooker; stir to blend. Add meatballs; turn to coat. Cover and cook on LOW 3 to 4 hours or on HIGH 1½ to 2 hours.

3. Meanwhile, cook pasta in large saucepan of salted boiling water according to package directions for al dente; drain. Serve sauce and meatballs with spaghetti. Garnish with basil.

CHEESY POLENTA ▸

MAKES 6 SERVINGS

- 6 cups vegetable broth
- 1½ cups uncooked medium-grind instant polenta
- ½ cup grated Parmesan cheese, plus additional for serving
- ¼ cup (½ stick) butter, cubed
- Fried sage leaves (optional; see note)

1. Bring broth to a boil in large saucepan over high heat. Pour into slow cooker; whisk in polenta.

2. Cover and cook on LOW 2 to 2½ hours or until polenta is tender and creamy. Stir in ½ cup cheese and butter. Serve with additional cheese. Garnish with sage.

NOTE

To fry sage, melt 1 tablespoon butter in small skillet over medium heat. Add sage leaves; cook 2 to 3 minutes or until crisp and lightly browned.

CREAMY CHICKEN SAUSAGE RICE PILAF

MAKES 6 TO 8 SERVINGS

- 1 package (about 4 ounces) wild rice
- ½ cup uncooked brown basmati rice
- 3 carrots, chopped
- 1 onion, chopped
- ½ cup dried cranberries
- 1 teaspoon dried oregano
- ¾ teaspoon salt
- 3 cups water
- 1 package (12 ounces) fully cooked chicken apple sausage, cut into ½-inch slices
- ½ cup whipping cream

1. Combine wild rice, brown rice, carrots, onion, cranberries, oregano and salt in slow cooker. Stir in water and sausage.

2. Cover and cook on LOW 7 to 8 hours or until rice is tender. Turn off heat. Stir in cream; let stand 10 minutes before serving.

HEARTY VEGETARIAN MAC AND CHEESE

MAKES 6 SERVINGS

- 8 ounces uncooked whole grain shell or penne pasta
- 1 can (about 14 ounces) stewed tomatoes, undrained
- 1½ cups jarred or refrigerated Alfredo sauce
- 1½ cups (6 ounces) shredded mozzarella cheese, divided
- 1 package (10 to 12 ounces) plant-based vegetarian sausage, cut into ¼-inch slices
- ¾ cup fresh basil leaves, thinly sliced, divided
- ½ cup vegetable broth
- ½ teaspoon salt
- 2 tablespoons grated Parmesan cheese

1. Cook pasta in large saucepan of salted boiling water 2 minutes less than package directs for al dente. Drain and place in slow cooker.

2. Add tomatoes, Alfredo sauce, 1 cup mozzarella cheese, sausage, ½ cup basil, broth and salt to slow cooker; stir to blend. Top with remaining ½ cup mozzarella cheese and Parmesan cheese.

3. Cover and cook on LOW 3½ hours or on HIGH 2 hours. Top with remaining ¼ cup basil.

ASIAGO AND ASPARAGUS RISOTTO-STYLE RICE

MAKES 4 SERVINGS

- 2 cups chopped onions
- 1 can (about 14 ounces) vegetable broth
- 1 cup uncooked converted rice
- 2 cloves garlic, minced
- 1 teaspoon salt
- ½ pound asparagus spears, trimmed and cut into 1-inch pieces
- ¾ cup half-and-half, divided
- ½ cup shredded Asiago cheese, plus additional for garnish
- ¼ cup (½ stick) butter, cut into pieces
- 2 ounces pine nuts or slivered almonds, toasted*

**To toast pine nuts, spread in single layer in heavy skillet. Cook and stir over medium heat 1 to 2 minutes or until nuts are lightly browned.*

1. Combine onions, broth, rice, garlic and salt in slow cooker; mix well. Cover and cook on HIGH 2 hours or until rice is tender.

2. Stir in asparagus and ½ cup half-and-half. Cover and cook on HIGH 20 to 30 minutes or until asparagus is crisp-tender.

3. Stir in ½ cup cheese, butter and pine nuts; cover and let stand 5 minutes to allow cheese to melt slightly. Fluff with fork and garnish with additional cheese before serving.

BEEFY TORTELLINI

MAKES 6 SERVINGS

- ½ pound ground beef
- 1 jar (24 to 26 ounces) roasted tomato and garlic pasta sauce
- 1 package (12 ounces) uncooked three-cheese tortellini
- 8 ounces sliced button or exotic mushrooms, such as oyster, shiitake and cremini
- ½ cup water
- ½ teaspoon red pepper flakes (optional)
- ¾ cup grated Asiago or Romano cheese
- Chopped fresh parsley (optional)

1. Spray inside of slow cooker with nonstick cooking spray. Brown beef in large skillet over medium-high heat 6 to 8 minutes, stirring to break up meat. Transfer to slow cooker using slotted spoon.

2. Stir pasta sauce, tortellini, mushrooms, water and red pepper flakes, if desired, into slow cooker.

3. Cover and cook on LOW 4 hours or on HIGH 2 hours, stirring halfway through cooking time. Top with cheese and parsley, if desired.

CHICKEN CACCIATORE

MAKES 6 SERVINGS

- 2 tablespoons olive oil, divided
- 1 medium onion, chopped
- 1 green bell pepper, chopped
- 1 package (8 ounces) sliced white or cremini mushrooms
- 1 teaspoon garlic powder
- 1 teaspoon dried rosemary
- ½ teaspoon salt
- ½ teaspoon dried thyme
- ½ teaspoon red pepper flakes
- 2 cans (about 14 ounces each) diced tomatoes with basil and oregano
- 1 can (6 ounces) tomato paste
- 6 boneless skinless chicken breasts (6 to 8 ounces each)
- Salt and black pepper
- 1 package (16 ounces) uncooked fettuccine or linguine

1. Heat 1 tablespoon oil in large skillet over medium-high heat. Add onion, bell pepper, mushrooms, garlic powder, rosemary, salt, thyme and red pepper flakes; cook and stir 5 to 7 minutes or until onion is softened. Transfer mixture to slow cooker. Stir in diced tomatoes and tomato paste.

2. Season chicken with salt and black pepper. Heat remaining 1 tablespoon oil in same skillet over medium-high heat. Add chicken; cook 3 to 5 minutes on each side until browned. Place in slow cooker. Cover and cook on LOW 6 hours.

3. Cook pasta in large saucepan of salted boiling water according to package directions for al dente. Drain and divide among serving bowls. Top with chicken and sauce.

CHEESE GRITS WITH CHILES AND BACON

MAKES 4 SERVINGS

- 6 slices bacon
- 1 to 2 serrano or jalapeño peppers, minced
- 1 large shallot or small onion, finely chopped
- 4 cups chicken broth
- 1 cup uncooked grits*
- ½ teaspoon salt
- ¼ teaspoon black pepper
- 1 cup (4 ounces) shredded Cheddar cheese
- ½ cup half-and-half
- 2 tablespoons finely chopped green onion

**Use coarse, instant, yellow or stone-ground grits.*

1. Cook bacon in medium skillet over medium heat until crisp, turning occasionally. Drain on paper towel-lined plate. Crumble two slices and place in slow cooker. Crumble and refrigerate remaining bacon.

2. Drain all but 1 tablespoon drippings from skillet. Return to medium heat. Add serrano pepper and shallot; cook and stir 2 minutes or until shallot is lightly browned. Transfer to slow cooker; stir in broth, grits, salt and black pepper. Cover and cook on LOW 4 hours.

3. Stir in cheese and half-and-half. Sprinkle with green onion and reserved bacon.

CLASSIC BEEF AND NOODLES

MAKES 6 SERVINGS

- 1 tablespoon vegetable oil
- 2 pounds cubed beef stew meat
- 1 package (8 ounces) sliced mushrooms
- ½ cup chopped onion
- 2 cloves garlic, minced
- 1 teaspoon salt
- 1 teaspoon dried oregano
- ½ teaspoon black pepper
- ¼ teaspoon dried marjoram
- 1 bay leaf
- 1½ cups beef broth
- ⅓ cup dry sherry
- 1 container (8 ounces) sour cream
- ½ cup all-purpose flour
- ¼ cup water
- 1 package (16 ounces) uncooked egg noodles
- Chopped fresh parsley

1. Heat oil in large skillet over medium heat. Brown beef in batches on all sides. Drain fat.

2. Combine beef, mushrooms, onion, garlic, salt, oregano, pepper, marjoram and bay leaf in slow cooker. Pour in broth and sherry. Cover and cook on LOW 8 to 10 hours or on HIGH 4 to 5 hours. Remove and discard bay leaf.

3. Combine sour cream, flour and water in small bowl. Whisk about 1 cup cooking liquid from slow cooker into sour cream mixture. Stir mixture into slow cooker. Cook, uncovered, on HIGH 30 minutes or until thickened and bubbly.

4. Meanwhile, cook noodles in large saucepan of salted boiling water according to package directions for al dente. Drain and divide among serving bowls. Top with beef mixture and parsley.

BARLEY WITH CURRANTS AND PINE NUTS ▸

MAKES 4 SERVINGS

- 1 tablespoon butter
- 1 onion, finely chopped
- 2 cups vegetable broth
- ½ cup uncooked pearl barley
- ½ teaspoon salt
- ¼ teaspoon black pepper
- ⅓ cup currants
- ¼ cup pine nuts

1. Melt butter in small skillet over medium-high heat. Add onion; cook 5 minutes or until lightly browned, stirring occasionally. Transfer to slow cooker. Add broth, barley, salt and pepper; stir in currants. Cover and cook on LOW 3 hours.

2. Stir in pine nuts; serve immediately.

BLACK BEANS AND RICE

MAKES 4 TO 6 SERVINGS

- 3 cups vegetable broth
- 1 can (15 ounces) black beans, rinsed and drained
- 1 can (15 ounces) whole kernel corn, drained
- 1¾ cups uncooked brown rice
- 1 teaspoon salt
- ½ teaspoon chili powder
- 1 cup salsa
- Optional toppings: shredded cheese, avocado slices, chopped fresh cilantro and/or sour cream

1. Combine broth, beans, corn, rice, salt and chili powder in slow cooker; mix well.

2. Cover and cook on HIGH 3 hours. Stir in salsa. Serve with desired toppings.

PIZZA CASSEROLE

MAKES 6 SERVINGS

- 1½ pounds ground beef
- 1 pound bulk pork sausage
- 4 jars (14 ounces each) pizza sauce
- 2 cups (8 ounces) shredded mozzarella cheese
- 2 cups grated Parmesan cheese
- 2 cans (4 ounces each) mushroom stems and pieces, drained
- 1 package (6 ounces) sliced pepperoni
- ½ cup finely chopped onion
- ½ cup finely chopped green bell pepper
- 1 clove garlic, minced
- 1 package (16 ounces) uncooked cellentani (corkscrew) pasta

1. Brown beef and sausage in large nonstick skillet over medium-high heat 6 to 8 minutes, stirring to break up meat. Transfer beef mixture to slow cooker using slotted spoon.

2. Add pizza sauce, cheeses, mushrooms, pepperoni, onion, bell pepper and garlic; stir to blend. Cover and cook on LOW 3½ hours or on HIGH 2 hours.

3. Cook pasta in large saucepan of salted boiling water according to package directions for al dente. Drain and stir into slow cooker. Cover and cook on HIGH 15 minutes or until pasta is heated through.

SPINACH RISOTTO

MAKES 4 SERVINGS

- 4 tablespoons butter, divided
- 1 tablespoon olive oil
- 2 shallots, finely chopped
- 1¼ cups uncooked Arborio rice
- ½ cup dry white wine
- 4 cups vegetable broth
- 1 teaspoon salt
- 2 cups baby spinach
- ¼ cup grated Parmesan cheese
- 2 tablespoons pine nuts, toasted*

**To toast pine nuts, spread in single layer in heavy skillet. Cook and stir over medium heat 1 to 2 minutes or until nuts are lightly browned.*

1. Melt 3 tablespoons butter in medium skillet over medium heat; add oil. Add shallot; cook and stir 5 minutes or until softened but not browned.

2. Add rice; cook and stir 2 minutes. Stir in wine; cook and stir until absorbed. Transfer to slow cooker. Stir broth and salt into slow cooker. Cover and cook on HIGH 2 to 2½ hours or until rice is al dente and a little liquid remains.

3. Stir in spinach. Cover and cook on HIGH 15 to 20 minutes or until rice is tender and creamy. Gently stir in cheese, pine nuts and remaining 1 tablespoon butter just before serving.

CHICKEN AND MUSHROOM FETTUCCINE ALFREDO

MAKES 6 TO 8 SERVINGS

- 1½ pounds chicken breast tenders
- 2 packages (8 ounces each) cremini mushrooms, cut into thirds
- ½ teaspoon salt
- ¼ teaspoon black pepper
- ¼ teaspoon garlic powder
- 2 packages (8 ounces each) cream cheese, cut into pieces
- 1½ cups grated Parmesan cheese, plus additional for garnish
- 1½ cups whole milk
- 1 cup (2 sticks) butter, cut into pieces
- 1 package (16 ounces) uncooked fettuccine
- Chopped fresh parsley

1. Spray inside of slow cooker with nonstick cooking spray. Arrange chicken in single layer in slow cooker. Top with mushrooms; sprinkle with salt, pepper and garlic powder.

2. Combine cream cheese, 1½ cups Parmesan cheese, milk and butter in medium saucepan over medium heat. Whisk constantly until smooth and heated through. Pour over mushrooms, pushing down any that float to surface. Cover and cook on LOW 4 to 5 hours or on HIGH 2 to 2½ hours.

3. Cook fettuccine in large saucepan of salted boiling water according to package directions for al dente; drain and stir into slow cooker. Garnish with additional Parmesan cheese and parsley.

MEXICAN-STYLE RICE AND CHEESE

MAKES 4 SERVINGS

- 1 can (about 15 ounces) Mexican-style beans
- 1 can (about 14 ounces) diced tomatoes with green chiles
- 2 cups (8 ounces) shredded Monterey Jack or Colby cheese, divided
- 1½ cups uncooked converted rice
- 1 large onion, finely chopped
- 4 ounces cream cheese, cut into pieces
- 3 cloves garlic, minced
- ½ teaspoon salt

1. Spray inside of slow cooker with nonstick cooking spray. Combine beans, tomatoes, 1 cup Monterey Jack cheese, rice, onion, cream cheese, garlic and salt in slow cooker; mix well.

2. Cover and cook on LOW 6 to 8 hours. Sprinkle with remaining 1 cup Monterey Jack cheese; cover and let stand until melted.

Vegetable Mains and Sides

BLACK BEAN, ZUCCHINI AND CORN ENCHILADAS

MAKES 6 SERVINGS

- 1 tablespoon vegetable oil
- 1 medium onion, chopped
- 1 medium zucchini, diced
- 1½ cups frozen corn
- 1 red bell pepper, chopped
- 1 teaspoon minced garlic
- ½ teaspoon salt
- ½ teaspoon ground cumin
- ¼ teaspoon ground coriander
- 1 can (about 15 ounces) black beans, rinsed and drained
- 3 cups salsa verde
- 12 (6-inch) corn tortillas
- 2½ cups (10 ounces) shredded Monterey Jack cheese
- 2 tablespoons chopped fresh cilantro

1. Heat oil in large skillet over medium heat. Add onion; cook and stir 5 minutes or until softened. Add zucchini, corn and bell pepper; cook and stir 2 minutes. Add garlic, salt, cumin and coriander; cook and stir 1 minute. Stir in beans. Remove from heat.

2. Pour 1 cup salsa into slow cooker. Arrange three tortillas in single layer, cutting the tortillas in half as needed to make them fit. Place one third of vegetable mixture over tortillas; sprinkle with ½ cup cheese. Repeat layering two more times. Layer with remaining three tortillas; top with 2 cups salsa. Sprinkle with remaining 1 cup cheese.

3. Cover and cook on HIGH 2 hours or until cheese is bubbly and edges are lightly browned. Sprinkle with cilantro. Turn off heat. Let stand, uncovered, 10 minutes before serving. Cut into squares to serve.

GERMAN POTATO SALAD ▸

MAKES 6 SERVINGS

- 8 slices bacon
- 1 medium onion, chopped
- 3 stalks celery, chopped
- 2 pounds small red potatoes, cut into ¼-inch slices
- 1 cup chicken broth
- ½ teaspoon salt
- ¼ cup cider vinegar
- Salt and black pepper

1. Cook bacon in large skillet over medium heat until crisp, turning occasionally. Drain bacon on paper towel-lined plate. Chop bacon; refrigerate until ready to serve. Return skillet with drippings to medium heat. Add onion and celery; cook and stir 6 to 8 minutes or until onion is softened.

2. Layer half of potatoes and half of onion mixture in slow cooker; repeat layers. Pour in broth and sprinkle with salt. Cover and cook on HIGH 4 hours. Stir in vinegar, bacon, salt and pepper.

CHEESY MASHED POTATOES

MAKES 10 TO 12 SERVINGS

- 4 pounds Yukon Gold potatoes, peeled and cut into 1-inch pieces
- 2 cups vegetable broth
- 3 tablespoons butter, cubed
- ½ cup milk
- ⅓ cup sour cream
- ½ teaspoon salt
- ¼ teaspoon black pepper
- 2 cups (8 ounces) shredded sharp Cheddar cheese

1. Spray inside of slow cooker with nonstick cooking spray. Add potatoes and broth; dot with butter. Cover and cook on LOW 4½ to 5 hours.

2. Mash potatoes with potato masher; stir in milk, sour cream, salt and pepper until blended. Stir in cheese until melted.

ZOODLES IN TOMATO SAUCE

MAKES 4 SERVINGS

- 1 can (28 ounces) diced tomatoes
- 1 can (6 ounces) tomato paste
- ¼ cup chopped onion
- 2 teaspoons minced garlic
- 1 teaspoon salt
- ½ teaspoon dried oregano
- ½ teaspoon dried basil
- 2 large zucchini (about 16 ounces each)*
- ¼ cup shredded Parmesan cheese (optional)

**Or substitute 2 pounds prepared zucchini noodles from the produce section of the supermarket.*

1. Spray inside of slow cooker with nonstick cooking spray. Add diced tomatoes, tomato paste, onion, garlic, salt, oregano and basil; stir to blend. Cover and cook on HIGH 3 hours.

2. Meanwhile, trim ends of zucchini and cut into 3-inch pieces. Spiral zucchini with fine spiral blade. Add zucchini to slow cooker. Cover and cook on HIGH 30 minutes or until zucchini is tender. Top with cheese, if desired.

BALSAMIC-HONEY GLAZED ROOT VEGETABLES

MAKES 6 SERVINGS

- 4 medium carrots, cut into ½-inch pieces
- 2 medium parsnips, cut into ¾-inch pieces
- 1½ pounds sweet potatoes, peeled and cut into 1-inch pieces
- 2 medium red onions, each cut through root end into 6 wedges
- ¼ cup honey
- 3 tablespoons butter, melted
- 1 tablespoon balsamic vinegar
- 1 teaspoon salt
- ¼ teaspoon black pepper

1. Combine carrots, parsnips, sweet potatoes, onions, honey, butter, vinegar, salt and pepper in slow cooker; toss to coat. Cover and cook on LOW 4 to 5 hours.

2. Transfer vegetables to large bowl using slotted spoon. Turn slow cooker to HIGH. Cover and cook on HIGH 15 minutes or until sauce is thickened. Return vegetables to slow cooker; toss to coat.

TWICE "BAKED" POTATOES

MAKES 4 SERVINGS

- 4 baking potatoes (about 10 ounces each)
- 3 tablespoons olive oil, divided
- 1 head garlic
- ¼ cup sour cream
- 1 to 2 tablespoons milk
- ½ teaspoon salt
- ¼ teaspoon black pepper
- 2 slices bacon, crisp-cooked and crumbled
- ½ cup (2 ounces) shredded Cheddar cheese, divided
- ¼ teaspoon smoked paprika
- Sliced green onions (optional)

1. Rub potatoes with 2 tablespoons oil; wrap each potato in foil. Place potatoes in slow cooker. Cut across top of garlic head. Place garlic in foil; top with remaining 1 tablespoon oil. Twist foil closed around garlic; place on top of potatoes. Cover and cook on HIGH 4 hours or until potatoes are soft when pierced with knife.

2. Pull foil away from each potato and crimp around bottoms. Cut thin slice from top of each potato. Scoop inside of potatoes into large bowl, leaving about ¼-inch shell. Squeeze garlic head to remove softened cloves; mash with fork. Measure 1 tablespoon mashed garlic; add to bowl with potatoes. Reserve remaining garlic in refrigerator for another use.

3. Add sour cream, milk, salt and pepper to potato mixture; beat with electric mixer at medium speed 3 to 4 minutes or until smooth. Stir in bacon and ¼ cup cheese. Spoon mashed potatoes into shells, mounding tops. Top with remaining ¼ cup cheese and paprika.

4. Return potatoes to slow cooker. Cover and cook on HIGH 15 minutes or until cheese is melted. Garnish with green onions.

CHILES RELLENOS

MAKES 3 TO 6 SERVINGS

- 6 whole poblano peppers
- 2½ cups (10 ounces) grated Chihuahua cheese or queso fresco, divided
- ½ cup plus 2 tablespoons salsa verde, divided
- ¼ cup plus 2 tablespoons chopped fresh cilantro, divided
- 1 (1-inch) piece serrano pepper
- 1 clove garlic
- 1 can (12 ounces) evaporated milk
- 2 eggs
- 2 tablespoons all-purpose flour
- ⅔ cup sour cream

1. Spray inside of slow cooker with nonstick cooking spray. Preheat broiler. Place peppers on baking sheet; broil about 4 inches from heat just until skins blister, turning occasionally. Place in paper bag or resealable food storage bag. Close bag; let stand 5 minutes. Scrape skin from peppers. Cut down one side of each pepper; open flat and remove any seeds or membranes. Pat dry with paper towels.

2. Divide 1½ cups cheese evenly among peppers; roll to enclose. Lay peppers in single layer in bottom of slow cooker.

3. Combine ½ cup salsa, ¼ cup cilantro, serrano pepper and garlic in food processor or blender; pulse until chopped. Add evaporated milk, eggs and flour; process until smooth. Pour over peppers. Top with remaining 1 cup cheese. Cover and cook on LOW 3 hours.

4. Combine sour cream and remaining 2 tablespoons salsa verde in small bowl. Serve peppers with sour cream mixture; sprinkle with remaining 2 tablespoons cilantro.

FRIJOLES BORRACHOS

MAKES 8 SERVINGS

- 6 slices bacon, chopped
- 1 medium yellow onion, chopped
- 1 tablespoon minced garlic
- 3 jalapeño peppers, seeded and finely diced
- 1 tablespoon dried oregano
- 1 can (12 ounces) beer
- 6 cups water
- 1 pound dried pinto beans, rinsed and sorted
- 1 can (about 14 ounces) diced tomatoes
- 1 tablespoon salt
- ¼ cup chopped fresh cilantro

1. Cook bacon in large skillet over medium heat 5 minutes or until crisp, stirring occasionally. Transfer bacon to slow cooker with slotted spoon. Drain all but 3 tablespoons drippings from skillet.

2. Return skillet to medium heat. Add onion; cook and stir 6 minutes or until softened and lightly browned. Add garlic, jalapeño peppers and oregano; cook 30 seconds or until fragrant. Increase heat to medium-high. Add beer; bring to a simmer. Cook 2 minutes, stirring to scrape up browned bits. Pour mixture into slow cooker.

3. Add water, beans, tomatoes and salt to slow cooker. Cover and cook on LOW 7 hours or on HIGH 3 to 4 hours. Mash beans slightly until broth is thickened and creamy. Top with cilantro.

THAI RED CURRY WITH TOFU

MAKES 4 SERVINGS

- 1 medium sweet potato, peeled and cut into 1-inch pieces
- 1 small eggplant, halved lengthwise and cut crosswise into ½-inch-wide halves
- 8 ounces extra firm tofu, cut into 1-inch pieces
- ½ cup cut green beans (1-inch pieces)
- ½ red bell pepper, cut into ¼-inch-wide strips
- 2 tablespoons vegetable oil
- 5 medium shallots, thinly sliced (about 1½ cups)
- 3 tablespoons Thai red curry paste
- 1 teaspoon minced garlic
- 1 teaspoon grated ginger
- 1 can (about 13 ounces) unsweetened coconut milk
- 1½ tablespoons soy sauce
- 1 tablespoon packed brown sugar
- ¼ cup chopped fresh basil
- 2 tablespoons lime juice
- Hot cooked rice

1. Spray inside of slow cooker with nonstick cooking spray. Add sweet potato, eggplant, tofu, green beans and bell pepper.

2. Heat oil in large skillet over medium heat. Add shallots; cook and stir 5 minutes or until browned and tender. Add curry paste, garlic and ginger; cook and stir 1 minute. Add coconut milk, soy sauce and brown sugar; bring to a simmer. Pour mixture over vegetables in slow cooker.

3. Cover and cook on LOW 2 to 3 hours. Stir in basil and lime juice. Serve with rice.

MASHED ROOT VEGETABLES

MAKES 6 SERVINGS

- 1 pound baking potatoes, peeled and cut into 1-inch pieces
- 1 pound turnips, peeled and cut into 1-inch pieces
- 12 ounces sweet potatoes, peeled and cut into 1-inch pieces
- 8 ounces parsnips, peeled and cut into ½-inch pieces
- 5 tablespoons butter, cut into pieces
- ¼ cup water
- 2 teaspoons salt
- ¼ teaspoon black pepper
- 1 cup milk

1. Spray inside of slow cooker with nonstick cooking spray. Add baking potatoes, turnips, sweet potatoes, parsnips, butter, water, salt and pepper; stir to blend. Cover and cook on HIGH 3 to 4 hours.

2. Mash vegetables with potato masher until smooth. Stir in milk. Cover and cook on HIGH 15 minutes.

PORTOBELLO BOLOGNESE SAUCE

MAKES 4 SERVINGS

- 2 tablespoons olive oil
- 2 cups chopped portobello mushrooms
- 4 cloves garlic, minced
- 1 jar (24 to 26 ounces) spicy pasta sauce
- 1 cup thinly sliced carrots
- 2 tablespoons tomato paste
- 12 ounces uncooked thin spaghetti
- ½ cup grated Parmesan or Romano cheese
- ¼ cup shredded fresh basil

1. Spray inside of slow cooker with nonstick cooking spray. Heat oil in large skillet over medium heat. Add mushrooms and garlic; cook and stir 6 minutes or until mushrooms have released their liquid.

2. Combine mushroom mixture, pasta sauce, carrots and tomato paste in slow cooker; stir to blend. Cover and cook on LOW 5 to 6 hours or on HIGH 2½ to 3 hours or until sauce has thickened and carrots are tender.

3. Cook spaghetti in large saucepan of salted boiling water according to package directions for al dente. Drain and divide among bowls; top with sauce, cheese and basil.

BRUSSELS SPROUTS WITH BACON, THYME AND RAISINS ▸

MAKES 8 SERVINGS

- 2 pounds Brussels sprouts, ends trimmed and cut in half lengthwise
- 1 cup chicken broth
- ⅔ cup golden raisins
- 2 thick slices applewood smoked bacon, chopped
- 2 tablespoons chopped fresh thyme
- Salt and black pepper

1. Combine Brussels sprouts, broth, raisins, bacon and thyme in slow cooker; mix well.

2. Cover and cook on LOW 3 to 4 hours. Season with salt and pepper.

CHUNKY RANCH POTATOES

MAKES 8 SERVINGS

- 3 pounds red potatoes, quartered
- 1 cup water
- ½ cup ranch dressing
- ½ cup grated Parmesan or Cheddar cheese
- ¼ cup minced fresh chives

1. Place potatoes and water in slow cooker. Cover and cook on LOW 7 to 9 hours or on HIGH 4 to 6 hours or until potatoes are tender.

2. Stir in ranch dressing, cheese and chives. Break up potatoes into chunks.

ASIAN KALE AND CHICKPEAS

MAKES 4 SERVINGS

- 1 tablespoon toasted sesame oil
- 1 medium onion, thinly sliced
- 2 teaspoons grated fresh ginger
- 2 cloves garlic, minced
- 2 jalapeño peppers, chopped
- 8 cups chopped kale
- 2 cans (about 15 ounces each) chickpeas, drained
- 1 cup vegetable broth
- ½ teaspoon salt
- 1 tablespoon lime juice
- 2 teaspoons soy sauce or fish sauce
- 1 teaspoon grated lime peel
- Hot cooked rice (optional)

1. Spray inside of slow cooker with nonstick cooking spray. Heat oil in large nonstick skillet over medium-high heat. Add onion, ginger, garlic and jalapeños; cook and stir 1 minute. Add kale; cook about 2 minutes, tossing until slightly wilted. Transfer mixture to slow cooker. Stir in chickpeas, broth and salt.

2. Cover and cook on LOW 3 hours or until kale is tender. Turn off slow cooker. Stir in lime juice, soy sauce and peel. Serve over rice, if desired.

RUSTIC GARLIC MASHED POTATOES ▸

MAKES 6 SERVINGS

- 2 pounds baking potatoes, cut into ½-inch cubes
- ¼ cup water
- 2 tablespoons butter, cut into small pieces
- 1¼ teaspoons salt
- ½ teaspoon garlic powder
- ¼ teaspoon black pepper
- 1 cup milk

1. Combine potatoes, water, butter, salt, garlic powder and black pepper in slow cooker; mix well. Cover and cook on LOW 7 hours or on HIGH 4 hours.

2. Add milk; mash potatoes with potato masher until smooth.

ASPARAGUS AND CHEESE SIDE DISH

MAKES 4 TO 6 SERVINGS

- 1 can (10½ ounces) cream of asparagus soup
- 1 can (10½ ounces) cream of celery or chicken soup
- 1 egg
- 1½ pounds fresh asparagus, trimmed
- 4 ounces American cheese, cut into cubes
- 2 cups crushed saltine crackers
- ⅔ cup slivered almonds

1. Combine soups and egg in slow cooker until well blended. Fold in asparagus and cheese. Top with crackers and almonds.

2. Cover and cook on HIGH 3 to 3½ hours or until asparagus is tender.

Sandwiches and Tacos

ITALIAN MEATBALL HOAGIES

MAKES 4 SERVINGS

- ½ pound ground beef
- ½ pound Italian sausage, casings removed
- ¼ cup seasoned dry bread crumbs
- ¼ cup grated Parmesan cheese, plus additional for topping
- 1 egg
- 1 tablespoon olive oil
- 1 cup pasta sauce
- 2 tablespoons tomato paste
- ¼ teaspoon red pepper flakes (optional)
- 4 (6-inch) hoagie rolls, split

1. Spray inside of slow cooker with nonstick cooking spray. Combine beef, sausage, bread crumbs, ¼ cup cheese and egg in large bowl; mix well. Shape into 12 (1½-inch) meatballs.

2. Heat oil in large skillet over medium heat. Add meatballs; cook 6 to 8 minutes or until browned on all sides, turning occasionally. Transfer to slow cooker using tongs.

3. Combine pasta sauce, tomato paste and red pepper flakes, if desired, in medium bowl; stir to blend. Spoon over meatballs; toss gently.

4. Cover and cook on LOW 5 to 7 hours or on HIGH 2½ to 3 hours. Serve meatballs in rolls with sauce and additional cheese.

TOFU, BLACK BEAN AND CORN CHILI BURRITOS

MAKES 10 SERVINGS

- 1 can (about 15 ounces) black beans, rinsed and drained
- 1 can (about 14 ounces) diced tomatoes with green pepper, celery and onion
- 8 ounces firm tofu, crumbled
- 1 cup mild salsa
- ¾ cup vegetable broth or water
- ½ cup frozen corn
- ½ cup uncooked white rice
- 1 tablespoon chili powder
- 1 teaspoon ground cumin
- 1 teaspoon salt
- ¼ teaspoon ground chipotle pepper
- ½ teaspoon dried oregano
- 10 large flour tortillas (8 to 10 inches)
- Optional toppings: sliced avocado, sour cream, lettuce and/or chopped fresh cilantro

1. Combine beans, tomatoes, tofu, salsa, broth, corn, rice, chili powder, cumin, salt, chipotle pepper and oregano in slow cooker; stir to blend. Cover and cook on LOW 8 hours or on HIGH 4 hours.

2. Top tortillas with bean mixture. Fold short ends of each tortilla over part of filling then roll up. Serve with desired toppings.

BARBECUED BEEF SANDWICHES

MAKES 12 SERVINGS

- 1 boneless beef chuck shoulder roast (about 3 pounds)
- 1 teaspoon salt
- 2 cups ketchup
- 1 medium onion, chopped
- ¼ cup cider vinegar
- ¼ cup molasses
- 2 tablespoons Worcestershire sauce
- 2 cloves garlic, minced
- ½ teaspoon dry mustard
- ½ teaspoon pepper
- ¼ teaspoon garlic powder
- ¼ teaspoon red pepper flakes
- Sesame seed buns, split

1. Cut roast in half; place in slow cooker. Sprinkle with salt. Combine ketchup, onion, vinegar, molasses, Worcestershire sauce, garlic, mustard, pepper, garlic powder and red pepper flakes in medium bowl until well blended. Pour over roast. Cover and cook on LOW 8 to 10 hours or on HIGH 4 to 5 hours.

2. Place roast on cutting board; cool slightly. Trim and discard excess fat; shred meat using two forks. Let sauce stand 5 minutes to allow fat to rise. Skim off fat. Return shredded meat to slow cooker; stir to coat with sauce.

3. Cover and cook 15 to 30 minutes or until heated through. Serve meat on buns.

CUBAN PORK SANDWICHES

MAKES 8 SERVINGS

- 1 pork loin roast (about 2 pounds)
- ½ cup orange juice
- 2 tablespoons lime juice
- 1 tablespoon minced garlic
- 1½ teaspoons salt
- ½ teaspoon red pepper flakes
- 2 tablespoons yellow mustard
- 8 crusty bread rolls, split in half (6 inches each)
- 8 slices Swiss cheese
- 8 thin ham slices
- 4 small dill pickles, thinly sliced lengthwise

1. Spray inside of slow cooker with cooking spray; add pork loin. Combine orange juice, lime juice, garlic, salt and red pepper flakes in small bowl. Pour over pork.

2. Cover and cook on LOW 7 to 8 hours or on HIGH 3½ to 4 hours. Place pork on cutting board; let stand until cool enough to handle. Cut into thin slices.

3. To serve, spread mustard on cut sides of rolls. Divide pork slices among roll bottoms. Top each with Swiss cheese slice, ham slice and pickles; cover with tops of rolls.

4. Spray large skillet with cooking spray; heat over medium heat. Working in batches, arrange sandwiches in skillet. Cover with foil and top with dinner plate to press down sandwiches. (If necessary, weigh down with 2 to 3 cans to compress sandwiches lightly.) Heat until cheese is slightly melted.* Serve immediately.

**Or use table top grill to compress and heat sandwiches.*

CHICKEN AND SPICY BLACK BEAN TACOS

MAKES 6 SERVINGS

- 1 can (about 15 ounces) black beans, rinsed and drained
- 1 can (10 ounces) diced tomatoes with mild green chiles, drained
- 1½ teaspoons chili powder
- 1 teaspoon olive oil
- ¾ teaspoon ground cumin
- ½ teaspoon salt
- 12 ounces boneless skinless chicken breasts
- 12 hard taco shells
- Optional toppings: shredded lettuce, diced tomatoes, shredded Cheddar cheese, sour cream and/or sliced black olives

1. Spray inside of slow cooker with nonstick cooking spray. Add beans and tomatoes with chiles. Combine chili powder, oil, cumin and salt in small bowl; rub all over chicken. Place chicken in slow cooker. Cover and cook on HIGH 1 to 2 hours.

2. Transfer chicken to large cutting board; cut into ½-inch slices. Scoop bean mixture into large bowl using slotted spoon.

3. To serve, warm taco shells according to package directions. Fill with bean mixture and chicken. Top as desired.

HOT BEEF SANDWICHES AU JUS

MAKES 8 TO 10 SERVINGS

- 4 pounds boneless beef bottom round roast, trimmed*
- 2 cans (about 10 ounces each) condensed beef broth
- 1 can (12 ounces) beer
- 2 envelopes (1 ounce each) onion soup mix
- 1 tablespoon minced garlic
- 2 teaspoons sugar
- 1 teaspoon dried oregano
- Crusty French rolls, sliced in half

**If your slow cooker is smaller than 5 quarts, cut any roast larger than 2½ pounds in half so it cooks completely.*

1. Place beef in slow cooker. Combine broth, beer, dry soup mix, garlic, sugar and oregano in large bowl; stir to blend. Pour mixture over beef. Cover and cook on HIGH 6 to 8 hours.

2. Transfer beef to large cutting board; shred with two forks. Return beef to cooking liquid; stir to blend. Serve on rolls with cooking liquid for dipping.

CHICKEN AND BRIE SANDWICHES

MAKES 6 SANDWICHES

- 1 red bell pepper, chopped
- 2 carrots, sliced
- ½ cup sliced celery
- 1 onion, chopped
- 1 clove garlic, minced
- ¼ teaspoon dried oregano
- ¼ teaspoon red pepper flakes
- ¼ cup all-purpose flour
- 1 teaspoon salt
- ½ teaspoon black pepper
- 6 boneless skinless chicken thighs
- 1 tablespoon vegetable oil
- 1 can (about 14 ounces) chicken broth
- 6 sub rolls, sliced in half and toasted *or* 2 thin baguettes (about 12 ounces each), sliced in half and toasted
- 1 large wedge brie cheese, cut into 12 pieces

1. Place bell pepper, carrots, celery, onion, garlic, oregano and red pepper flakes in slow cooker.

2. Combine flour, salt and black pepper in large bowl. Working in batches, coat chicken with flour mixture. Heat oil in large skillet over medium-high heat; brown chicken on both sides.

3. Place chicken over vegetables in slow cooker; add broth. Cover and cook on LOW 5 to 6 hours.

4. Transfer chicken to cutting board. Slice and place on sub rolls; drizzle with broth mixture and top with cheese, vegetables and tops of rolls.

TIP

To serve these sandwiches as sliders, cut them into thirds and secure with toothpicks.

ANCHO CHILE AND LIME PORK TACOS

MAKES 10 TO 12 SERVINGS

- 2 large plantain leaves
- 1 pork shoulder roast or pork chops (4 to 6 pounds)*
- Juice of 4 limes
- 1 package (about 1 ounce) ancho chile paste
- 1 teaspoon salt
- 1 large onion, sliced
- Pickled Red Onions (recipe follows)
- Flour tortillas
- Optional toppings: salsa, sour cream, guacamole, shredded cheese, lime slices and/or hot pepper sauce

**If your slow cooker is smaller than 5 quarts, cut any roast larger than 2½ pounds in half so it cooks completely.*

1. Line slow cooker with plantain leaves; top with pork roast. Combine lime juice, chile paste and salt in medium bowl; stir until well blended. Spread paste mixture over pork; top with onion and wrap leaves over pork. Cover and cook on LOW 8 to 10 hours.

2. Meanwhile, prepare Pickled Red Onions.

3. Serve pork in tortillas with Pickled Red Onions and desired toppings.

PICKLED RED ONIONS

Combine 1 cup sliced red onion and juice from 1 to 2 limes in small bowl; set aside until juice is absorbed. Makes 1 cup.

PULLED PORK SLIDERS WITH COLA BARBECUE SAUCE

MAKES 16 SLIDERS

- 1 boneless pork shoulder roast (3 pounds)*
- Salt and black pepper
- 1 tablespoon vegetable oil
- 1 cup cola beverage
- ¼ cup tomato paste
- 2 tablespoons packed brown sugar
- 2 teaspoons Worcestershire sauce
- 2 teaspoons spicy brown mustard
- Hot pepper sauce
- 16 dinner rolls or potato rolls, split
- Sliced pickles (optional)

**If your slow cooker is smaller than 5 quarts, cut any roast larger than 2½ pounds in half so it cooks completely.*

1. Season pork all over with salt and black pepper. Heat oil in large skillet over medium-high heat. Add pork; cook until browned on all sides. Place in slow cooker. Pour cola over pork. Cover and cook on LOW 7½ to 8 hours or on HIGH 3½ to 4 hours.

2. Turn off heat. Transfer pork to large cutting board; shred with two forks. Let cooking liquid stand 5 minutes. Skim off and discard fat. Whisk tomato paste, brown sugar, Worcestershire sauce and mustard into cooking liquid. Cover and cook on HIGH 15 minutes or until thickened.

3. Stir shredded pork back into slow cooker. Season with hot pepper sauce. Serve on rolls with pickles, if desired.

CHIPOTLE SLOPPY JOE SLIDERS

MAKES 12 SLIDERS

- 1 pound turkey or pork Italian sausage links, casings removed
- 1 package (14 ounces) frozen green and red bell pepper strips with onions
- 1 can (6 ounces) tomato paste
- 1 tablespoon quick-cooking tapioca
- 1 tablespoon minced canned chipotle peppers in adobo sauce, plus 1 tablespoon sauce
- 2 teaspoons ground cumin
- ½ teaspoon dried thyme
- 12 corn muffins or small dinner rolls, split and toasted

1. Brown sausage in large skillet over medium-high heat 6 to 8 minutes, stirring to break up meat. Transfer to slow cooker using slotted spoon.

2. Stir in pepper strips with onions, tomato paste, tapioca, chipotle peppers with sauce, cumin and thyme. Cover and cook on LOW 8 to 10 hours. Serve on corn muffins.

ITALIAN BEEF ▸

MAKES 8 SERVINGS

- 1 beef rump roast (3 to 5 pounds)*
- 2 cups mild giardiniera
- 1 can (14 ounces) beef broth
- 8 Italian sandwich rolls

**If your slow cooker is smaller than 5 quarts, cut any roast larger than 2½ pounds in half so it cooks completely.*

1. Place roast in slow cooker; add giardiniera and broth. Cover and cook on LOW 10 hours.

2. Shred beef; serve on rolls with sauce.

TAVERN BURGER

MAKES 8 SERVINGS

- 2 pounds ground beef
- ½ cup ketchup
- ¼ cup packed brown sugar
- ¼ cup yellow mustard
- Hamburger buns

1. Brown beef in medium skillet over medium-high heat 6 to 8 minutes, stirring to break up meat. Drain fat. Transfer beef to slow cooker. Add ketchup, brown sugar and mustard to slow cooker; mix well.

2. Cover and cook on LOW 4 to 6 hours. Serve on buns.

Appetizers and Dips

HONEY-GLAZED CHICKEN WINGS

MAKES 6 SERVINGS

- 3 tablespoons vegetable oil, divided
- 3 pounds chicken wings
- 1 cup honey
- ½ cup soy sauce
- 2 tablespoons tomato paste
- 2 teaspoons water
- 1 clove garlic, minced
- 1 teaspoon sugar
- 1 teaspoon black pepper

1. Heat 1½ tablespoons oil in large skillet over medium heat. Add wings in batches; cook until browned on all sides. Place chicken in slow cooker.

2. Combine remaining 1½ tablespoons oil, honey, soy sauce, tomato paste, water, garlic, sugar and pepper in medium bowl; whisk until well blended. Pour sauce over wings. Cover and cook on LOW 6 to 8 hours or on HIGH 3 to 4 hours.

PEPPERONI PIZZA MONKEY BREAD

MAKES 12 SERVINGS

- ½ (6-ounce) package pepperoni, divided
- 1 teaspoon minced garlic
- ¼ teaspoon red pepper flakes
- 1 can (about 16 ounces) refrigerated biscuits
- 1 can (15 ounces) pizza sauce
- 1 red bell pepper, chopped
- 2 cups (8 ounces) shredded mozzarella cheese

1. Spray inside of slow cooker with nonstick cooking spray. Prepare foil handles (see note). Spray foil handles with cooking spray.

2. Chop half of pepperoni. Combine chopped pepperoni, garlic and red pepper flakes in medium bowl. Cut each biscuit into six pieces. Roll each biscuit piece into pepperoni mixture; place in slow cooker. Top with half of pizza sauce; reserve remaining sauce for serving. Top sauce with bell pepper, cheese and remaining half of pepperoni slices.

3. Cover and cook on LOW 3 hours. Turn off heat; let stand 10 to 15 minutes. Remove from slow cooker using foil handles. Serve with remaining pizza sauce for dipping.

NOTE

Prepare foil handles by tearing off one 18-inch long piece of foil; fold in half lengthwise. Fold in half lengthwise again to create 18×3-inch strip. Repeat two times. Crisscross foil strips in spoke design; place in slow cooker.

FOCACCIA WITH ROSEMARY AND ROMANO

MAKES 8 TO 10 SERVINGS

- 1¼ cups warm water (100° to 110°F)
- 1 packet (¼ ounce) active dry yeast
- 1 tablespoon sugar
- 3 to 3½ cups all-purpose flour
- 1½ tablespoons finely chopped fresh rosemary
- 2 teaspoons salt
- ½ teaspoon red pepper flakes
- 3 tablespoons olive oil
- ¼ cup grated Romano cheese

1. Spray inside of slow cooker with nonstick cooking spray. Combine water, yeast and sugar in small bowl; let stand 5 minutes or until frothy.

2. Combine 3 cups flour, rosemary, salt and red pepper flakes in large bowl. Add yeast mixture and oil; stir until soft dough forms. Turn out dough onto lightly floured surface; knead 5 minutes or until dough is smooth and elastic, adding additional flour by tablespoons if needed to prevent sticking.* Place dough in slow cooker; stretch to fit bottom. Cover and let rise 1 hour until doubled in size.

3. Gently deflate dough with fingertips. Sprinkle with cheese. Cover and let rise 30 minutes. Place clean, dry towel over top of slow cooker; replace lid. Cover and cook on HIGH 2 hours or until bread is lightly browned around edge. Remove to wire rack; cool at least 10 minutes before slicing.

**To knead dough, fold dough in half toward you and press dough away from you with heels of hands. Give dough a quarter turn and continue folding, pushing and turning. Or use a stand mixer fitted with dough hook. Knead at low speed 5 minutes.*

SPICY CHEDDAR DIP

MAKES ABOUT 3 CUPS

- 4 slices bacon, chopped
- 1 package (8 ounces) cream cheese, cubed
- 2 cups (8 ounces) shredded extra sharp Cheddar cheese
- 1 jalapeño pepper, finely chopped
- 1 teaspoon hot pepper sauce
- 6 tablespoons sour cream
- Tortilla chips and pretzel sticks

1. Cook bacon in medium skillet over medium heat until crisp, stirring occasionally. Transfer to paper towel-lined plate with slotted spoon.

2. Spray inside of slow cooker with nonstick cooking spray. Combine cream cheese, Cheddar cheese, jalapeño, hot pepper sauce and bacon in slow cooker.

3. Cover and cook on LOW 1 hour. Stir in sour cream. Cover and cook 30 minutes or until heated through and cheese is melted. Serve with tortilla chips and pretzel sticks.

BARBECUE SLOPPY JOE DIP

MAKES ABOUT 1½ CUPS

- 2 teaspoons olive oil
- 1 pound ground beef
- ½ cup finely chopped onion
- 1 clove garlic, minced
- ¼ teaspoon dried oregano
- ¼ cup barbecue sauce
- 2 tablespoons ketchup
- 2 teaspoons packed brown sugar
- 2 teaspoons cider vinegar
- ¾ cup (3 ounces) shredded Monterey Jack cheese
- 1 tablespoon chopped fresh cilantro
- Baguette slices

1. Heat oil in large skillet over medium-high heat. Add beef; cook and stir 6 to 8 minutes or until browned. Add onion, garlic and oregano; cook and stir 4 minutes. Remove from heat. Stir in barbecue sauce, ketchup, brown sugar and vinegar. Let cool 2 minutes; stir in cheese.

2. Transfer to slow cooker. Cover and cook on LOW 1 hour or until cheese is melted. Stir well; sprinkle with cilantro. Serve with baguette slices.

HERBED OLIVE LOAF

MAKES ABOUT 12 SERVINGS

- 1 cup warm water (100° to 110°F)
- 3 tablespoons olive oil
- 3 packages (¼ ounce each) active dry yeast
- 1 tablespoon sugar
- 3 cups all-purpose flour
- ½ cup pitted kalamata olives, chopped
- 1 tablespoon plus 2 teaspoons chopped fresh rosemary, divided
- 1 teaspoon salt
- ¼ teaspoon red pepper flakes

1. Combine water, oil, yeast and sugar in medium bowl; let stand 5 minutes. Combine flour, olives, 1 tablespoon rosemary and salt in large bowl. Add yeast mixture; stir until rough dough forms. Turn out dough onto floured surface; knead about 5 to 6 minutes or until smooth and elastic.*

2. Place dough in large lightly greased bowl; turn to grease top. Cover and let rise in warm place about 1½ hours or until doubled in size.

3. Spray inside of slow cooker with nonstick cooking spray. Place dough in slow cooker; press and stretch to fit. Sprinkle with remaining 2 teaspoons rosemary and red pepper flakes.

4. Cover and cook on HIGH 1½ to 2 hours or until bread is puffed and lightly browned around edge. Remove to wire rack; cool at least 10 minutes before cutting into wedges.

**To knead dough, fold dough in half toward you and press dough away from you with heels of hands. Give dough a quarter turn and continue folding, pushing and turning. Or use a stand mixer fitted with dough hook. Knead at low speed 5 minutes.*

SPICY SWEET AND SOUR COCKTAIL FRANKS ▸

MAKES 10 TO 12 SERVINGS

- 1 package (14 ounces) cocktail franks
- ½ cup ketchup or chili sauce
- ½ cup apricot preserves
- 1 teaspoon hot pepper sauce

Combine cocktail franks, ketchup, preserves and hot pepper sauce in slow cooker; mix well. Cover and cook on LOW 1 to 2 hours.

ARTICHOKE AND NACHO CHEESE DIP

MAKES ABOUT 4 CUPS

- 2 cans (10½ ounces each) nacho cheese soup
- 1 can (14 ounces) quartered artichoke hearts, drained and coarsely chopped
- 1 cup (4 ounces) shredded or thinly sliced pepper Jack cheese
- 1 can (4 ounces) evaporated milk
- 2 tablespoons minced fresh chives, divided
- ½ teaspoon paprika
- Crackers or chips

1. Combine soup, artichokes, cheese, evaporated milk, 1 tablespoon chives and paprika in slow cooker. Cover and cook on LOW 2 hours.

2. Stir well; sprinkle with remaining 1 tablespoon chives. Serve with crackers.

APRICOT AND BRIE DIP ▸

MAKES 3 CUPS

- ½ cup dried apricots, finely chopped
- ⅓ cup plus 1 tablespoon apricot preserves, divided
- ¼ cup apple juice
- 2 pounds Brie cheese, rind removed and cut into cubes
- Assorted crackers

1. Combine apricots, ⅓ cup apricot preserves and apple juice in slow cooker. Cover and cook on HIGH 40 minutes.

2. Stir in cheese. Cover and cook on HIGH 30 minutes or until cheese is melted. Stir in remaining 1 tablespoon preserves. Serve dip with crackers.

MAPLE-GLAZED MEATBALLS

MAKES 12 SERVINGS

- 2 packages (about 16 ounces each) frozen fully cooked meatballs, partially thawed and separated
- 1 can (20 ounces) pineapple chunks packed in juice, drained
- 1½ cups ketchup
- 1 cup maple syrup
- ⅓ cup soy sauce
- 1 tablespoon quick-cooking tapioca
- 1 teaspoon dry mustard
- ½ teaspoon ground allspice

1. Combine meatballs, pineapple, ketchup, maple syrup, soy sauce, tapioca, mustard and allspice in slow cooker; mix well.

2. Cover and cook on LOW 5 to 6 hours. Stir before serving.

FETA AND MINT SPREAD ▸

MAKES ABOUT 1 CUP

- ½ cup plain Greek yogurt
- 3 ounces feta cheese, crumbled
- 2 ounces cream cheese, cubed
- 2 tablespoons olive oil
- 1 clove garlic, minced
- 1 tablespoon chopped fresh mint
- ½ teaspoon grated fresh lemon peel
- Pita chips

1. Spray inside of slow cooker with nonstick cooking spray. Add yogurt, feta cheese, cream cheese, oil and garlic; mix well. Cover and cook 1 hour or until cheese is melted.

2. Stir in mint and lemon peel. Serve spread with pita chips.

CHIPOTLE CHILI CON QUESO DIP

MAKES 1½ CUPS

- 10 ounces pasteurized process cheese product, cubed
- ¼ cup mild chunky salsa
- 1 to 2 canned chipotle peppers in adobo sauce,* finely chopped
- ½ teaspoon Worcestershire sauce
- ⅛ teaspoon chili powder
- Pretzel twists or rods

**Use more to taste.*

1. Spray inside of slow cooker with nonstick cooking spray. Combine cheese product, salsa, chipotle pepper, Worcestershire sauce and chili powder in slow cooker. Cover and cook on LOW 1 hour.

2. Stir well. Cover and cook on LOW 30 minutes or until cheese product is melted. Stir until well blended. Serve dip with pretzels.

PEPPERONI PIZZA DIP

MAKES 1⅓ CUPS

- 1 jar (about 14 ounces) pizza sauce
- ⅓ cup chopped pepperoni
- ½ can (about 2¼ ounces) sliced black olives, drained
- 1 teaspoon dried oregano
- ½ cup (2 ounces) shredded mozzarella cheese
- 4 ounces cream cheese, softened
- Bread sticks

1. Combine pizza sauce, pepperoni, olives and oregano in slow cooker; stir to blend. Cover and cook on LOW 1 hour.

2. Stir in mozzarella cheese and cream cheese. Cover and cook on LOW 30 minutes or until cheese is melted. Stir until well blended. Serve dip with bread sticks.

BARBECUED MEATBALLS

MAKES 12 SERVINGS

- 2 pounds ground beef
- 1⅓ cups ketchup, divided
- 1 egg
- 3 tablespoons seasoned dry bread crumbs
- 2 tablespoons dried onion flakes
- ¾ teaspoon garlic salt
- ½ teaspoon black pepper
- 1 cup packed brown sugar
- 1 can (6 ounces) tomato paste
- ¼ cup soy sauce
- ¼ cup cider vinegar
- 1½ teaspoons hot pepper sauce

1. Preheat oven to 350°F. Combine beef, ⅓ cup ketchup, egg, bread crumbs, onion flakes, garlic salt and black pepper in large bowl. Mix gently but thoroughly; shape into 1-inch meatballs.

2. Arrange meatballs in single layer on two 15×10-inch baking pans. Bake 18 minutes or until browned. Transfer meatballs to slow cooker.

3. Combine remaining 1 cup ketchup, brown sugar, tomato paste, soy sauce, vinegar and hot pepper sauce in medium bowl. Pour over meatballs. Cover and cook on LOW 4 hours.

CARAMELIZED ONION DIP

MAKES ABOUT 3 CUPS

- 2 tablespoons olive oil
- 3 cups chopped sweet onions
- 2 teaspoons sugar
- ¼ teaspoon dried thyme
- ½ teaspoon salt
- 4 ounces cream cheese, cubed
- 1 cup sour cream
- ⅔ cup mayonnaise
- ⅔ cup shredded Swiss cheese
- Potato chips and carrot sticks

1. Heat oil in large skillet over medium heat. Add onions, sugar and thyme; cook 20 minutes or until golden, stirring occasionally. Stir in salt.

2. Spray inside of slow cooker with nonstick cooking spray. Add onion mixture, cream cheese, sour cream, mayonnaise and Swiss cheese. Cover and cook on LOW 30 minutes. Stir until well blended. Serve dip with potato chips and carrot sticks.

Desserts and Drinks

BANANA PECAN BREAD PUDDING

MAKES 10 TO 12 SERVINGS

- 4 eggs
- 2¼ cups whipping cream, divided
- ½ cup plus 2 tablespoons sugar, divided
- 2 teaspoons vanilla
- 1 loaf (1 pound) cinnamon swirl bread, cut into cubes
- 3 small bananas, cut into ¾-inch-thick slices
- ½ cup chopped pecans
- ¼ cup maple syrup
- 2 tablespoons butter

1. Spray inside of slow cooker with nonstick cooking spray. Whisk eggs in large bowl until well blended. Add 2 cups cream, ½ cup sugar and vanilla; whisk until blended. Add bread, bananas and pecans; mix well. Let stand 5 minutes. Pour into slow cooker. Cover and cook on LOW 2½ to 3 hours or until center is set.

2. For glaze, combine remaining ¼ cup cream, maple syrup, butter and remaining 2 tablespoons sugar in small saucepan. Cook and stir over low heat 4 to 5 minutes or until butter is melted and sugar is dissolved. Let cool 5 minutes. Serve over bread pudding.

BAKED FUDGE PUDDING CAKE

MAKES 6 TO 8 SERVINGS

- 6 tablespoons unsweetened cocoa powder
- ¼ cup all-purpose flour
- ⅛ teaspoon salt
- 4 eggs
- 1⅓ cups sugar
- 1 cup (2 sticks) butter, melted and cooled
- 1 teaspoon vanilla
- Grated peel of 1 orange
- ½ cup whipping cream
- Chopped toasted pecans, whipped cream or vanilla ice cream

1. Spray inside of slow cooker with nonstick cooking spray. Whisk cocoa, flour and salt in small bowl.

2. Beat eggs in large bowl with electric mixer at medium-high speed until thickened. Gradually add sugar, beating about 5 minutes or until very thick and pale yellow. Add butter, vanilla and orange peel; beat until blended. Stir in cocoa mixture. Add cream; mix until blended. Pour batter into slow cooker.

3. Lay clean kitchen towel or paper towels across top of slow cooker; cover with lid. Cook on LOW 3 to 4 hours. Sprinkle with pecans; serve with whipped cream.

FRENCH TOAST BREAD PUDDING

MAKES 6 TO 8 SERVINGS

- 2 tablespoons packed dark brown sugar
- 2½ teaspoons ground cinnamon
- 1 loaf (24 ounces) Texas toast-style bread*
- 2 cups whipping cream
- 2 cups half-and-half
- 2 teaspoons vanilla
- ¼ teaspoon salt
- 4 egg yolks
- 1¼ cups granulated sugar
- ¼ teaspoon ground nutmeg
- Maple syrup
- Whipped cream (optional)

**If unavailable, cut day-old 24-ounce loaf of white sandwich bread into 1-inch-thick slices.*

1. Spray inside of slow cooker with nonstick cooking spray. Combine brown sugar and cinnamon in small bowl. Reserve 1 tablespoon for topping; set aside.

2. Cut bread slices in half diagonally. Arrange bread slices in single layer in bottom of slow cooker, keeping as flat as possible. Evenly sprinkle with rounded tablespoon of cinnamon mixture. Repeat layering with remaining bread and cinnamon mixture, keeping layers as flat as possible. Tuck bread into vertical spaces, if necessary.

3. Bring cream, half-and-half, vanilla and salt to a boil in large saucepan over medium heat, stirring frequently. Reduce heat to low.

4. Meanwhile, whisk egg yolks and granulated sugar in medium bowl. Whisking constantly, gradually add ¼ cup hot cream mixture in thin steady stream. Stir mixture back into saucepan. Increase heat to medium; cook and stir about 5 minutes or until mixture thickens slightly. Do not boil.

5. Remove from heat; stir in nutmeg. Pour mixture over bread and press bread down lightly. Sprinkle with reserved cinnamon mixture. Cover and cook on LOW 3 to 4 hours or on HIGH 1½ to 2 hours or until toothpick inserted into center comes out clean.

6. Turn off slow cooker. Remove cover; let stand 10 minutes. Serve with maple syrup and whipped cream, if desired.

PEACH COBBLER ▸

MAKES 4 TO 6 SERVINGS

- 2 packages (16 ounces each) frozen peaches, thawed and drained
- ¾ cup plus 1 tablespoon sugar, divided
- 2 teaspoons ground cinnamon, divided
- ½ teaspoon ground nutmeg
- ¾ cup all-purpose flour
- ⅛ teaspoon salt
- 6 tablespoons butter, cut into pieces
- Whipped cream (optional)

1. Combine peaches, ¾ cup sugar, 1½ teaspoons cinnamon and nutmeg in slow cooker.

2. For topping, combine flour, remaining 1 tablespoon sugar, remaining ½ teaspoon cinnamon and salt in small bowl. Cut in butter with pastry blender or fingertips until mixture resembles coarse crumbs. Sprinkle over peach mixture.

3. Cover and cook on HIGH 2 hours. Serve with whipped cream, if desired.

BANANA-RUM CUSTARD WITH VANILLA WAFERS

MAKES 5 SERVINGS

- 1½ cups milk
- 3 eggs
- ½ cup sugar
- 3 tablespoons dark rum *or* 2 teaspoons vanilla
- ⅛ teaspoon salt
- 1 medium banana, sliced ¼ inch thick
- 15 to 18 vanilla wafers

1. Beat milk, eggs, sugar, rum and salt in medium bowl. Pour into 1-quart soufflé dish or baking dish that fits in slow cooker. Do not cover.

2. Place rack in slow cooker and pour in 1 cup water. Place soufflé dish on rack. Cover and cook on LOW 3½ to 4 hours.

3. Remove dish from slow cooker. Top individual servings with banana slices and wafers.

APPLE-PECAN BREAD PUDDING

MAKES 8 SERVINGS

- 8 cups bread, cubed
- 3 cups Granny Smith apples, cubed
- 1 cup chopped pecans
- 8 eggs
- 1 can (12 ounces) evaporated milk
- 1 cup packed brown sugar
- ½ cup apple cider or apple juice
- 2 teaspoons ground cinnamon
- 1 teaspoon ground nutmeg
- 1 teaspoon vanilla
- ½ teaspoon salt
- ½ teaspoon ground allspice
- Vanilla ice cream (optional)
- Caramel topping (optional)

1. Spray inside of slow cooker with nonstick cooking spray. Add bread, apples and pecans.

2. Whisk eggs in large bowl until well blended. Add evaporated milk, brown sugar, apple cider, cinnamon, nutmeg, vanilla, salt and allspice; whisk until well blended. Pour into slow cooker.

3. Cover and cook on LOW 3 hours. Serve with ice cream and caramel topping, if desired.

STICKY CARAMEL PUMPKIN CAKE

MAKES 8 SERVINGS

- 2 cups all-purpose flour
- 2 teaspoons baking powder
- 1 teaspoon baking soda
- ½ teaspoon salt
- ½ teaspoon pumpkin pie spice or ground cinnamon
- 1⅓ cups sugar
- 1 cup (2 sticks) butter, softened
- 4 eggs, at room temperature
- 1 can (15 ounces) pumpkin purée
- 1 jar (16 ounces) caramel topping
- Vanilla ice cream (optional)

1. Spray inside of 5-quart slow cooker with nonstick cooking spray.

2. Whisk flour, baking powder, baking soda, salt and pumpkin pie spice in medium bowl. Beat sugar and butter in large bowl with electric mixer at high speed 3 minutes or until blended. Add eggs, one at a time, beating until well blended after each addition. Beat in pumpkin. Gradually add flour mixture at low speed until smooth. Spread evenly in slow cooker.

3. Cover and cook on HIGH 2 to 2½ hours or until toothpick inserted into center of cake comes out clean. Drizzle caramel topping over cake and serve with ice cream, if desired.

CHOCOLATE CHIP LEMON LOAF

MAKES 8 SERVINGS

- 1⅔ cups all-purpose flour
- 1½ teaspoons baking powder
- ¼ teaspoon salt
- ¾ cup granulated sugar
- ½ cup shortening
- 2 eggs
- ¾ cup milk
- ½ cup chocolate chips
- Grated peel of 1 lemon
- Juice of 1 lemon
- ¼ to ½ cup powdered sugar
- Melted chocolate (optional)

1. Spray 2-quart soufflé dish or baking dish that fits in slow cooker with nonstick cooking spray. Whisk flour, baking powder and salt in medium bowl.

2. Beat granulated sugar and shortening in large bowl until blended. Add eggs, one at a time, beating well after each addition. Add flour mixture alternately with milk, beating well after each addition. Stir in chocolate chips and lemon peel. Spoon batter into prepared dish. Cover with greased foil. Place in slow cooker.

3. Cook, covered, with slow cooker lid slightly ajar to allow excess moisture to escape, on LOW 3 to 4 hours or on HIGH 1 hour 45 minutes to 2 hours or until edges are golden and knife inserted into center of loaf comes out clean. Remove dish from slow cooker; remove foil. Cool completely on wire rack.

4. Combine lemon juice and ¼ cup powdered sugar in small bowl until smooth. Add additional sugar as needed to reach desired glaze consistency. Pour glaze over loaf. Drizzle loaf with melted chocolate, if desired.

MINTED HOT COCOA ▸

MAKES 6 TO 8 SERVINGS

- 6 cups milk
- ¾ cup semisweet chocolate pieces
- ½ cup sugar
- ½ cup unsweetened cocoa powder
- 1 teaspoon vanilla
- ½ teaspoon mint extract
- 10 fresh mint sprigs, tied together with kitchen string, plus additional for garnish
- Whipped cream (optional)

1. Combine milk, chocolate, sugar, cocoa, vanilla and mint extract in slow cooker; stir to blend. Add 10 mint sprigs. Cover and cook on LOW 3 to 4 hours.

2. Uncover; remove and discard mint sprigs. Whisk cocoa mixture well; cover until ready to serve. Garnish each serving with whipped cream and additional mint sprigs.

HOT TODDIES

MAKES 10 SERVINGS

- 8 cups water
- ¾ cup honey
- ⅔ cup lemon juice
- 1 (1-inch) piece fresh ginger, peeled and cut into 4 slices
- 1 whole cinnamon stick
- 2 cups bourbon
- Lemon slices (optional)

1. Combine water, honey, lemon juice, ginger and cinnamon stick in slow cooker; stir to blend. Cover and cook on HIGH 2 hours. Turn slow cooker to WARM.

2. Remove and discard cinnamon stick and ginger pieces. Stir in bourbon. Garnish each serving with lemon slices.

GINGER PEAR CIDER ▸

MAKES 8 TO 10 SERVINGS

- 8 cups pear juice or cider
- ¾ cup lemon juice
- ¼ to ½ cup honey
- 10 whole cloves
- 2 cinnamon sticks, plus additional for garnish
- 8 (¼-inch) slices fresh ginger

1. Combine pear juice, lemon juice, honey, cloves, 2 cinnamon sticks and ginger in slow cooker.

2. Cover and cook on LOW 5 to 6 hours or on HIGH 2½ to 3 hours. Remove and discard cloves, cinnamon sticks and ginger before serving. Garnish with additional cinnamon sticks.

MOCHA SUPREME

MAKES 8 SERVINGS

- 2 quarts strong brewed coffee
- ½ cup instant hot chocolate beverage mix
- 1 whole cinnamon stick, broken in half
- 1 cup whipping cream
- 1 tablespoon powdered sugar

1. Place coffee, hot chocolate mix and cinnamon stick halves in slow cooker; stir. Cover and cook on HIGH 2 to 2½ hours or until heated through. Remove and discard cinnamon stick halves.

2. Beat cream in medium bowl with electric mixer on high speed until soft peaks form. Add powdered sugar; beat until stiff peaks form. Serve coffee topped with whipped cream.

Index

Index

Q

R

S

Metric Conversion Chart

VOLUME MEASUREMENTS (dry)

1/8 teaspoon = 0.5 mL
1/4 teaspoon = 1 mL
1/2 teaspoon = 2 mL
3/4 teaspoon = 4 mL
1 teaspoon = 5 mL
1 tablespoon = 15 mL
2 tablespoons = 30 mL
1/4 cup = 60 mL
1/3 cup = 75 mL
1/2 cup = 125 mL
2/3 cup = 150 mL
3/4 cup = 175 mL
1 cup = 250 mL
2 cups = 1 pint = 500 mL
3 cups = 750 mL
4 cups = 1 quart = 1 L

VOLUME MEASUREMENTS (fluid)

1 fluid ounce (2 tablespoons) = 30 mL
4 fluid ounces (1/2 cup) = 125 mL
8 fluid ounces (1 cup) = 250 mL
12 fluid ounces (1 1/2 cups) = 375 mL
16 fluid ounces (2 cups) = 500 mL

WEIGHTS (mass)

1/2 ounce = 15 g
1 ounce = 30 g
3 ounces = 90 g
4 ounces = 120 g
8 ounces = 225 g
10 ounces = 285 g
12 ounces = 360 g
16 ounces = 1 pound = 450 g

DIMENSIONS

1/16 inch = 2 mm
1/8 inch = 3 mm
1/4 inch = 6 mm
1/2 inch = 1.5 cm
3/4 inch = 2 cm
1 inch = 2.5 cm

OVEN TEMPERATURES

250°F = 120°C
275°F = 140°C
300°F = 150°C
325°F = 160°C
350°F = 180°C
375°F = 190°C
400°F = 200°C
425°F = 220°C
450°F = 230°C

BAKING PAN SIZES

Utensil	Size in Inches/Quarts	Metric Volume	Size in Centimeters
Baking or Cake Pan (square or rectangular)	8×8×2	2 L	20×20×5
	9×9×2	2.5 L	23×23×5
	12×8×2	3 L	30×20×5
	13×9×2	3.5 L	33×23×5
Loaf Pan	8×4×3	1.5 L	20×10×7
	9×5×3	2 L	23×13×7
Round Layer Cake Pan	8×1½	1.2 L	20×4
	9×1½	1.5 L	23×4
Pie Plate	8×1¼	750 mL	20×3
	9×1¼	1 L	23×3
Baking Dish or Casserole	1 quart	1 L	—
	1½ quart	1.5 L	—
	2 quart	2 L	—